Mum knows best

Mum knows best

Exceedingly helpful household hints

M & J Hanks

◨ SQUARE PEG

Published by Square Peg 2011

6 8 10 9 7

First published in Great Britain in 2011 by
Square Peg
Random House, 20 Vauxhall Bridge Road,
London SW1V 2SA

www.randomhouse.co.uk

Addresses for companies within The Random House Group can be found at:
www.randomhouse.co.uk/offices.htm

The Random House Group Limited Reg. No. 954009

A CIP catalogue record for this book
is available from the British Library

ISBN 9780224086851

The Random House Group Limited supports The Forest Stewardship
Council® (FSC®), the leading international forest-certification organisation.
Our books carrying the FSC label are printed on FSC®-certified paper.
FSC is the only forest-certification scheme supported by the leading
environmental organisations, including Greenpeace. Our
paper procurement policy can be found at
www.randomhouse.co.uk/environment

This book contains general guidance on and suggestions for the use of household
products. This book is not a substitute and not to be relied on for specific advice and
readers must refer to the relevant manufacturers' and/or service providers' instructions
and precautions. So far as the authors are aware the information given is correct and up
to date as at March 2011. Practice, laws and regulations all change, and the reader
should obtain up to date professional advice on any such issues. The authors and
publishers disclaim, as far as the law allows, any liability arising directly or indirectly
from the use, or misuse, of the information contained in this book.

Typeset in Bell Gothic Light by Palimpsest Book Production Limited,
Falkirk, Stirlingshire
Printed and bound in Great Britain
by Clays Ltd, St Ives plc

For Rosalind Hanks and Elizabeth Kennedy,
two mums who definitely know best.

Contents

Introduction

Though concerned with all things domestic, this book is not about how to be a good little housewife. Rather, it is a book for mums, dads, sons and daughters. For cousins, aunties, grandmothers and great-grandmothers. In short, it's a book for anyone who gets up everyday, dresses themselves and has a life to get on with. It is not a drab list of instructions for the modern house-holder, but a volume to be dipped in and out of, a cele-bration of good, old-fashioned, homegrown wisdom, a 'two fingers' to the drab world of overpriced products and gizmos for every household task. The title is a nod to the fact that, historically, it was women who domi-nated the domestic realm, and generations of mums who devised canny, economical and often ingenious ways to do what had to be done. Nowadays, many people live alone, stay-at-home dads are becoming more common, and most people agree that dividing up the chores is only fair. However, in many cases, mum still knows best.

As husband and wife, we've always been rather clue-less when it came to knowing how to fit in cleaning, washing, cooking and general house-holding into our busy lives. Once we found the time, knowing how to get the jobs done correctly was another problem entirely.

More often than not, we'd grab some supermarket-bought spray or other and wipe around in a hurry until everything looks spick, but perhaps not span! And whenever we didn't know how to do something, we'd call one of our mums, who always seemed to know the answer. Researching this book opened our eyes to vast tracts of helpful and memorable tips for so many aspects of domestic life. Some are amusing, some thoroughly complicated, and some beautifully simple. There were many 'I wish I'd known that when...' moments, and much fun trying out some of the more bizarre sounding tips (it only seemed fair to our potential readers).

We hope that the tips and wrinkles within will brighten up the life of anyone who reads on. They've certainly changed the way we live.

Mark and Joanna Hanks

2011

Spick and Span
Essential Cleaning Tips

General

Clean silver in a hurry
Using a cloth, apply methylated spirits. Allow to dry for a minute or two, then polish. Works on glass too.

Banana skins on silver
Liquidise banana skins in your food processor. The paste is fabulous for shining silver.

Rubber darkens silver
So take your Marigolds off when polishing.

Brass doorknobs and other household brass fittings
Many ordinary household products can be used to bring a pristine shine to lacklustre brass fittings in the home:

▶ **Tomato ketchup** – squeeze a drop onto a clean, soft cloth and rub over the brass. After a few minutes, wipe clean with a rinsed cloth, using another soft, dry cloth, polish to a shine.

▶ **Worcestershire or HP sauce** – use as with the ketchup method above, rinsing the item carefully until clean before shining with a dry cloth.

▶ **White vinegar and salt** – mix a tablespoon of salt with enough white vinegar to make a loose paste. Apply the paste to the brass with a cloth, allow to work its magic for a minute or two before rinsing off with a clean cloth.

▶ **Yoghurt** – coat the brass in yoghurt and leave to dry before buffing to a shine with a clean, dry cloth.

▶ **Lemons or limes** – dip half a lemon or lime in salt and rub all over the brass.

▶ Rinse the object with a damp, hot cloth and finish by polishing to a shine with a clean, soft, dry cloth.

▶ Brasso is a great way to clean brass, of course, but an initial rub with ammonia will make the job of cleaning neglected brass even easier!

Old wives' brass-cleaning tip

Save your bean water and drop hard-to-clean, fiddly pieces of brass into it.

Copper

As above, dip half a lemon or lime in salt – it will clean copper items beautifully. Rinse the item in/with hot water, dry, then polish to a shine with a clean, soft cloth. For old or badly stained copper, dip in a solution of Harpic in water. When the copper colour begins to change, remove and rinse. Finish by polishing as usual.

Toothpaste on metal and white leather
Toothpaste is great on most metals and white leather in the absence of specific cleaners.

Place bent playing cards in the microwave
Plastic-coated playing cards will straighten out with a quick blast in the microwave.

Don't forget to dust light bulbs
A clean bulb gives out twice as much light as a dirty one.

Tomato stains on Tupperware
To avoid those annoying stains on plastic, coat the insides of containers with vegetable oil before pouring in sauces containing tomato.

Home-made brass and copper cleaner
Mix together two egg whites, a glass of vinegar, two tablespoons of plain flour and throw in a pinch of salt. Rub onto brass or copper and leave for fifteen minutes before rinsing with warm water.

Chalk kept in a drawer

Will absorb moisture and stop silver cutlery from tarnishing as quickly.

Spring cleaning

Start at the top of the house, and work gradually towards your front door. Don't lock yourself out. . . .

Never use soap on stone floors

It leaves scum in its wake. Rub with washing soda instead and rinse with warm water.

Fabulous floor polish

Can be made as follows: Place a couple of wax candles (or the equivalent in saved candle stubs) and 225 grams of leftover soap into quarter of a pint (150 millilitres) of boiling water. Mix well, and leave to cool. Now add quarter of a cup each of turpentine and linseed oil, and stir for a couple of minutes. Keep in a screw-top jar and shake before use.

Remove rust

By rubbing with salt and lemon juice.

Dustpan care

For a dustpan that allows the dust to slide gracefully into the bin, clean it and spray with furniture polish. Buff well. When your plastic dustpan and brush need a good clean, squeeze them in alongside the dirty plates in your dishwasher.

Use a potato for scouring

A cut potato dipped in baking soda makes an excellent scourer, especially when it comes to removing rust.

A cup of vinegar in your dishwasher and washing machine

Will keep them clean and odour-free and will also get rid of any limescale build-up. Once every few months is fine.

Customise your broom

Nailing a strip of draught excluder around your broom head will prevent damage to your skirting boards.

Cod liver oil

Will treat scratches on polished wood. Apply to damaged area, wait until it has soaked in fully and then polish in the usual manner.

Cold tea

Waste not want not. Save it for cleaning varnished floors
and they will come up a treat. Tannin in the tea helps
eliminate grease and bring out the natural colour of the
wood.

Old polish

Remove built-up layers of polish with a chamois leather
dipped in a solution of one part vinegar to eight parts
warm water. Wring out chamois well before rubbing, and
dry with a soft cloth.

For a longer lasting broom

Soak it in hot salt water. Once solution is cool, allow to
dry naturally. You have just extended the life of your
bristles.

Wrap in cotton wool

Slight dents in wooden furniture may improve if you lay
damp cotton wool over them for a few hours. This
encourages the wood to swell up and return to its original
shape.

Burns on wooden furniture

Silver polish removes the scorch marks.

Squirt shaving foam on your upholstery

As an emergency cleaner. Rub in gently with a dry cloth and sponge off with a wet one. Dry with kitchen roll.

Dull tiled and vinyl floors

If your floor remains dull even after a good mopping, add a cup of vinegar to some warm water and give it one more go . . .

Fashion a floor polisher

Simply wrap a duster around an old soft broom.

Good glass

Is no friend of the dishwasher. Wash the old-fashioned way, and add vinegar to rinsing water for that extra sparkle.

Rusty Brillo pads

Need not be so. To prevent rust forming, keep pads wrapped in tin foil when not in use.

Seriously stained sinks

Line the offending area with kitchen roll and cover in bleach. After half an hour, you may remove the towels. The stains will wipe away easily.

Rusty stainless steel

Will respond well to a good rub with a firelighter.
For other stains, try methylated spirits or white vinegar.

Clean your cards right

A brisk rub with a slice of bread is ideal for dirty, greasy
playing cards.

Extraordinary sofa-cleaning technique

Take a sheet large enough to cover your sofa or armchair,
and immerse in warm water. Wring sheet as dry as you
can, then drape over your item of furniture. Beat
thoroughly with a rolling pin or similar. The dust will rise
and stick to the sheet.

Hot dish marks on a table

Simmer a pint (600 millilitres) of linseed oil for ten
minutes, then add a quarter-pint (150 millilitres) of
turpentine. Apply frequently, and rub off with a soft cloth.
Alternatively, make a paste of salt and olive oil and coat
marks thickly. Leave for an hour, then polish as normal.
The stains should have disappeared.

Paint flecks on windows or marble

Rub off with the edge of a coin, or use a pencil eraser.

Baby-wipe your keyboard

Computer keyboards harbour many a germ – keep yours clean with baby wipes, which are cheaper than computer wipes and just as effective.

Scratch-free furniture

Scratches can be hidden with wax crayon or shoe polish of the same colour. Rub in and smooth over, leave for a while and then polish.

A good home-made furniture polish

Mix equal parts turpentine, methylated spirits, vinegar and paraffin. Shake in a bottle, apply to furniture with a soft cloth, then polish with a duster for an excellent finish with hardly any elbow grease.

Economical cleaning

Bars of soap will last much longer if, once you have opened the packet, the contents are left to dry out for a week before use.

Cut steel wool pads in half

They will go twice the distance.

Quality washing-up liquid
> Will be just as effective when diluted with water. A
> fifty:fifty ratio is about right.

Save used tin foil
> Give it a wash, then screw it up and use as a fantastic
> scourer.

Your rubber gloves
> Will wear quickest in the hand you use most. To wear them
> down evenly, and make them last longer, turn gloves inside
> out and wear them on opposite hands from time to time.

Dried-out shoe polish needn't be binned
> Pop it in the oven on a low heat. Before long it will be soft
> again.

Blow-dry your radiator!
> To clean an old-fashioned radiator, hang a damp towel
> down the back and use your hairdryer (on a cool setting)
> to blow through the gaps. Dust will gather on the towel.

Dirt on wallpaper
> A gentle rub with stale bread will remove many an
> undesired mark from your walls.

Start from the bottom and work up
When washing a wall, do so from the bottom upwards,
rinsing as you go along. If you start at the top, dirty
water streaks will run down the uncleaned sections.

For beautiful windows
Mix equal parts water, paraffin and methylated spirits in a
bottle. Shake up, apply to window with newspaper and rub.
Polish with a cloth for sparkling panes.

Water marks on wood
Rub a small amount of mayonnaise, butter or
margarine onto affected area. Leave overnight and
wipe off.

To clean mahogany
Dust first, then apply the following solution: one
tablespoon each of turpentine and linseed oil in two pints
(1.2 litres) of warm water. Polish well. Alternatively, hot
beer or hot tea (without milk) may be applied before
polishing.

To clean oak
Wash oak with warm water and allow to dry. In the
meantime, boil up a pint (600 millilitres) of beer, a small

nugget of beeswax and two to three teaspoons of sugar. Use a soft brush to apply. Once dry, polish with a chamois leather.

To clean teak
Rub down once a year with very fine (00 grade) wire wool. Polish with beeswax.

Drains and sinks
Flush all sinks and drains with a solution of water and bicarbonate of soda every week. This will help prevent unpleasant smells and blockages.

Salt and vinegar
Are good on taps and plugholes, as well as fish and chips. A vigorous rub will banish brown marks and leave them gleaming.

Clean windows on a dull day
Sunlight dries windows a little too quickly, leaving the panes of glass smeared.

Waste-disposal unit

To sharpen and clean the blades, pop some ice cubes into the unit, turn the tap on and switch on the unit. Throw in a sliced-up lemon for extra freshness.

Mincing tip

To get your mincer clean after mincing, put some stale bread through it.

China and teacups

Tea stains and other discolorations of china are easily cleaned by rubbing with kitchen salt and a little water. Once the stains are removed, wash as usual in soapy water.

Stair sweeping

Try using a soft, medium-sized paintbrush to get into awkward corners and rails. Then vacuum, or sweep into dustpan.

Fabric lampshades

Dip into warm soapy water and brush carefully with a soft brush. Rinse under a lukewarm tap, and stand to dry.

Kitchen

For a dirty microwave
Place several lemon slices into a bowl of water and cook on high for a few minutes. The steam will loosen the muck (which should be wiped clean) and give your microwave a fresh smell.

Kitchen sponges in the dishwasher
Damp, warm kitchen sponges are the perfect place for bacteria to fester and multiply. Often we unwittingly end up spreading germs instead of cleaning. Guard against this by regularly popping your sponges in the dishwasher. Peg them to the top rack to ensure they don't get caught at the bottom.

'Hairdry' your freezer
To speed up the defrosting process. Make sure your freezer doesn't defrost behind your back by investing in a buzzplug with a built-in alarm that sounds if the power fails or the fuse blows.

For easy freezer defrosting next time
Once your freezer has defrosted, lay a couple of sheets of waxed paper on the bottom shelf before plugging back in.

The next time you come to do the job, the ice will come away so much quicker.

Washing up efficiently

Hot water will cook eggs, cheese and breadcrumbs onto pans, making them difficult to remove. Rinse all cooking utensils, pots, pans and plates that have been in contact with these foods in cold water before putting them into your washing-up water or dishwasher. To remove burnt food from a casserole or pie dish, fill it with cold water and add a few drops of household bleach. Leave overnight and wash up as usual. Alternatively, fill the dish with cold tea and soak overnight.

Can't get the smell of fish off your silver?

Add a teaspoon of mustard powder to the washing-up water.

Prevention is better than cure

Keep the bottom of your oven and grill pan clean by laying down a sheet of tin foil and changing regularly. Oven shelves can also be covered. Stained or burnt oven shelves should be placed overnight in a bath – enough hot water to cover shelves and a few tablespoons of biological washing powder will loosen the muck.

Easy oven cleaning

Turn your oven on full power and leave for thirty minutes. Much of the dirt will simply burn off. Once the oven is cool enough, wipe clean with a heated damp cloth. Make sure you leave your windows open while you do this . . .

Cleaning an oven after use

After a particularly large or messy cooking or baking session, it can be worthwhile to clean the oven before the muck gets a chance to take hold. Turn the oven off and place a little bowl of household ammonia on the top shelf and a large bowl of boiling water on the bottom shelf. Shut the oven door, and reopen the next morning. Once you've removed the bowls, and allowed a few minutes for the smell to clear, clean the oven with soapy water, then rinse with warm water and leave to dry.

HARD HANDS FROM HOUSEWORK?

Give your fingers a treat by rubbing in a teaspoon of sugar and a teaspoon of olive oil. Stains and discoloration after cooking and chopping will vanish if you rub coffee grounds, a slice of raw potato or lemon slices into your digits.

RUB DRY MUSTARD IN YOUR HANDS

To get rid of the smell after chopping onions and garlic.

Bicarbonate of soda on oven walls

After you've cleaned an oven, it is always worthwhile rubbing some bicarbonate of soda paste on the oven walls. This will make the oven so much easier to clean the next time. Two tablespoons of soda in two tablespoons of boiling water will make a good paste.

Marble-ous cleaning tips

Douse stained marble with lemon juice, leave for a few seconds, and rinse off quickly. Add shine to coloured marble with colourless wax.

To rejuvenate dull and dirty marble

Mix one part powdered chalk, one part powdered pumice and two parts bicarbonate of soda with enough water to make a paste. Spread on with a paintbrush, and leave overnight. Wash away with lukewarm water and a soft brush.

Burnt roasting tins

Soak overnight in water and three tablespoons of washing detergent (the stuff you normally use for clothes). Wash as normal in the morning, and all should be well.

Burnt aluminium saucepans

Fill the pan with water and add a peeled onion. Place on a stove and bring to the boil. The burnt bits will soon come loose and rise to the surface of the water.

Use a stained saucepan

To cook rhubarb. That way you'll have something delicious and your pan should be free of stains.

Non-stick pan stains

Will disappear in a jiffy if you boil up a cup of water with two tablespoons of bicarbonate of soda and half a cup of vinegar. Simmer in the pan for fifteen minutes, drain and wash with soapy water.

Teapot no-nos

Never use washing soda to clean aluminium or copper teapots. Clean inside stains with fine wire wool. Keep pots away from damp places, as dampness will encourage chromium plating to peel.

Aluminium pan gone dark?

Add two teaspoons of cream of tartar to two pints (1.2 litres) of water and bring to the boil.

An earthenware casserole

Should be seasoned before first use. Rub the outside with a cut onion or a clove of garlic. Seasoning strengthens earthenware and allows higher temperatures when cooking. To avoid cracking, avoid pouring boiling liquid into your casserole unless you have warmed it first by running it under a warm tap.

Don't wash earthenware

In soap or detergent, as it will be absorbed. Hot water with salt or vinegar will achieve great results.

For an easy-clean cheese grater

Rub it lightly with vegetable oil before use, and the cheese will not stick.

After cooking fish

To eliminate fishy smells, sprinkle pan with used tea leaves and leave for 15 minutes before you wash up.

Bathroom

Dirty shower curtain

Remove curtain and place in washing machine. Fill
detergent drawer with your usual detergent, and in
addition pour a cup of white vinegar into your fabric
softener drawer. To remove stubborn mildew, rub curtain
with lemon juice. Soaking your curtain afterwards in
salted water will stop it coming back.

Denture tablets in a toilet

Stubborn stains in your toilet bowl will often disappear if
you drop in a few denture tablets and leave overnight.
Scrub and flush in the morning.

Dirty marks round the bath

To clean tidemarks on an enamel bath, lightly scour with a
damp cloth dipped in salt. Prevent tidemarks from
forming in the first place by adding a splash of washing-up
liquid to your bathwater. You'll get a bubble bath out of it,
too.

Treat a dirty bath to a good soaking

Fill to the brim with very hot water and add a few cups of
washing powder. Pull the plug after a couple of hours, and

give the bath a good rub-down with a cloth. Rinse with
warm water.

Remove build-up on shower heads and taps

Fill half a small plastic bag with screwed-up kitchen roll.
Pour in white vinegar until the paper is drenched. Place
the bag over the shower head or tap, making sure the
vinegar paper covers the scaly areas. Tie up the bag,
leave overnight, and by morning the limescale will peel
away.

POWDER YOUR MARIGOLDS

A sprinkle of talcum powder or baking soda inside
any rubber gloves will make them so much easier to
get on and off.

Sink detox

Every once in a while, it's a good idea to fill your sink
with piping hot water and a few capfuls of bleach. Once
water is at a temperature you can tolerate, don a rubber
glove and remove plug, quickly replacing it upside down.
The water should drain slowly, giving the overflow and
underside of plug a good clean.

Vaseline on your curtain rail
Will make sure your shower curtain keeps running without catching.

Hot vinegar in the bath
Pour hot vinegar around your bath to remove hard watermarks, stains from dripping taps and lingering limescale. Neat vinegar will remove most limescale from tiles.

Pour your cola down the loo
Leave for a few hours for a sparkling toilet bowl, and be glad you spared your teeth!

Sponges
Natural sponges respond very nicely to a good wash in vinegar and warm water. Rinse well in cold water and hang on the washing line to dry.

Stains in the toilet bowl
Mix borax and lemon juice into a paste and apply to stubborn marks for great results.

Clean a toilet at night
That way the bowl can soak until the first flush of the morning.

Soap dish tip

Clean your soap dish and apply a layer of baby oil to it.
Oil repels water, so makes it easier to keep clean.

Irons and Kettles

No more furry kettles

To prevent a kettle from furring up, put a clean oyster
shell in it. This will attract the chalky deposit away from
the inside of the kettle.

Boil up some vinegar

To descale your kettle. Last thing at night, add equal parts
vinegar and water to kettle, bring to the boil. After boiling,
leave overnight before cleaning out the mess, then rinse
well with cold water.

Basic iron cleaning

Sprinkle Vim onto a piece of newspaper and place on the
ironing board. Switch iron to high and iron over the
newspaper with a bit of pressure for fantastic results!

Remove starch marks

Rub a bar of soap on the iron while still hot, then polish off with a cloth.

Sticky iron remedy

Unplug and allow to cool. Dip a soft cloth in methylated spirits, or vinegar, and rub.

Glass

Glass bottles and decanters

Soak in a bowl of warm soapy water for twenty minutes and then rinse. Pour a handful of rice into the decanter, half-fill with malt vinegar or warm soapy water, then agitate gently. This should remove any cloudy film or persistent stains from the inside of the glass.
Alternatively, try using crushed eggshells shaken in the bottle when half-filled with warm water. This will clean it superbly.

A sparkling vase

Is easily achieved. Fill the dirty vase with warm water and add two denture-cleaning tablets. After a night's rest, the filth will simply wash off when rinsed.

Cutlery and Utensils

A rusty knife

Can be restored using an onion. Stick the rusty area into a large peeled onion. Move the blade back and forth to consign the problem to history.

Egg-stained spoons

Should be soaked in the water the eggs were boiled in. This will remove stubborn stains.

Blunt scissors around a bottleneck

Will sharpen them. Draw blades back and forth as if trying to cut through the glass. Cutting sandpaper also does the job.

White bone knife handles

To clean dissolve a little salt in some lemon juice and rub onto the handle with a soft rag. Rinse, then polish with a clean, soft cloth.

Smelly chopping knives

Wash in cold water if you have been chopping garlic or onions.

Blockages

Blocked drains, toilets and sinks

To instantly clear a badly blocked toilet or sink, pour a
caustic soda solution down the offending area. Great care
must be taken when using caustic soda. Wear gloves and
goggles, and read the instructions carefully, always adding
the caustic soda to the bucket of water. Never add the
water to the caustic soda!

Keep your drains running

Pour half a cup of washing soda down the sink, then add a
cup of white vinegar. After fifteen minutes, top it all off
with a kettle's worth of boiling water.

Over a Hot Stove
Cooking and Baking Hints

Peel your cheese
> A potato peeler is great for thin slices of cheese.

Freeze bread and kitchen roll
> Place a sheet or two of kitchen roll in the bag when freezing bread. That way, the roll will absorb moisture when you thaw the bread, and your loaf will be nice and dry.

No more dripping ice-cream cones
> Drop a small amount of peanut butter into an ice-cream cone to prevent the end going soggy and the ice cream dripping out of the bottom.

Nutcrackers on ice
> Use a nutcracker to break ice into pieces that will fit into a Thermos flask. For crushed ice, bag your cubes and smash with a rolling pin or the heel of your shoe.

Coffee in gravy
> A tiny sprinkling of instant coffee is a good substitute when you have run out of gravy browning.

Add a pinch of salt to coffee
> Strong overbrewed percolated coffee can be improved with a pinch of salt.

Eggshells in your espresso

Adding crushed eggshells to your ground coffee when brewing takes away the bitterness. Apparently.

Stop sausages rolling in the pan

Cook sausages in pairs by holding them together with toothpicks. They will cook more evenly and are easily flipped over.

Bag up a cookbook

A freezer bag over an open cookbook lets you read about your ingredients without spreading them onto the page.

Egg in your coffee

If one is short of milk, it's said that a dash of well-beaten egg is a reasonable substitute. Add egg to cup, then pour coffee and stir well. Try it, if you dare.

Turn your cream sour

Double cream mixed with lemon juice works as a substitute if you need sour cream in a hurry.

Chopping board tend to slip?

Make sure it stays in place by wrapping two elastic bands across each end of the board.

Decant all red wine and allow to breathe

Even cheap wine will improve in taste if opened, decanted and allowed to breathe for a couple of hours before consumption.

Efficient oven heating

Wait two minutes after turning your oven on and open the door for a couple of seconds. Any moist air will escape and the ventilation will greatly speed up heating time.

Make your own hotplate

Put a brick on your gas hob until hot. The brick will hold the heat for a surprisingly long time, and save on energy.

Stuck ketchup

If, after much shaking and tapping, your ketchup (or other sauces and creams) won't come out of a newly opened bottle, insert a drinking straw. A very gentle blow will encourage airflow, and sauceflow too.

Deep-frying hint

To lessen the amount of fat absorbed by your food, add a
tablespoon of vinegar to the fat just before frying.

Peeling

Soak potatoes or carrots in water for fifteen minutes
before peeling. Scrub with a stiff brush and the skin will
come off very easily. If you have peeled your potatoes in
advance of their cooking time, prevent them from going
brown by covering with water and half a cup of milk.

To prevent a pan boiling over

Add a small knob of butter to the water when cooking
rice, pasta, vegetables etc.

FOR PERFECT POPCORN WITH NO BURNT BITS

Ingredients

Three tablespoons rapeseed, groundnut or grapeseed
oil (high smoke-point oil)
One-third of a cup of high-quality popcorn kernels
Two tablespoons or more (to taste) of butter
Salt to taste

Method

1. Heat the oil in a large saucepan or pasta pan on medium high heat.

2. Put three or four popcorn kernels into the oil and cover the pan.

3. When the kernels pop, add remaining popcorn kernels to make an even layer. Cover, remove from heat and count thirty seconds. This brings all of the other kernels to a near-popping temperature so that when they are put back on the heat, they all pop at about the same time.

4. Return the pan to the heat. The popcorn will begin popping all at once. Once the popping starts in earnest, gently shake the pan by moving it back and forth over the hob. Try to keep the lid slightly ajar to release the steam from the popcorn (the popcorn will be drier and crisper). Once the popping slows to several seconds between pops, remove the pan from the heat, lift off the lid, and dump the popcorn immediately into a wide bowl.

5. Add butter and/or salt to taste.

Pour cornflour on spilt spaghetti

If you have dropped a pan of spaghetti on the kitchen floor, a good sprinkling of cornflour will stop it sliding all over the place as you attempt to pick it up.

LID ON OR OFF . . . ? THE RULES OF BOILING

For vegetables that grow above ground – lid off.
For those that grow below – lid on.
Simple.

Scissors rather than a knife

Sometimes scissors are much more efficient for cutting food than a knife. Try snipping raisins and other dried fruit, or the rind from bacon, and time will be on your side. Scissors can also be useful for dividing up a pizza in a flash and for removing fish heads. . . .

Mustard and Marmite in sandwiches

Try adding the condiment to the butter before spreading. This avoids overwhelmingly strong patches of mustard or Marmite and ensures an even distribution of flavour.

Leftover white wine

Can be added to the vinegar bottle.

Stuck lids

Metal lids on jars will expand under a hot tap, making them easy to twist off. If this does not work, wind an elastic band round the edge of the lid, then twist. If that fails too, pierce jar lid to release vacuum and transfer contents to another container.

Clothes pegs

Are just as good as expensive gadgets for sealing food bags and packets.

Mince your sandwich fillings

Minced or grated meat and cheese will go further if mixed with a dollop or two of mayonnaise.

Emergency! How To . . .

Rescue a dodgy home-made mayonnaise

► Put a teaspoon of mustard into a fresh bowl and add the mayonnaise gradually, beating vigorously until all is added.

▸ Separate a fresh egg yolk into a clean bowl, add the mayonnaise and beat until homogenous.

▸ If the oil and vinegar have separated, immediately add half a pinch of salt and an extra dessertspoonful of vinegar.

Revive a limp lettuce

Wash well, shake, wrap in a cloth and refrigerate for an hour. Alternatively, soak lettuce for 30 minutes in cold water in which a teaspoon of sugar has been dissolved.

Freshen rancid cooking oil

Add ground charcoal to the oil – 50 grams to every 500 millilitres of the stale oil. Replace the bottle lid and shake energetically for about five minutes before straining through a clean muslin or dishcloth.

Banish lingering food smells

Place a small bowl of white vinegar next to your cooking area.

Boil milk without burning

Place a large marble in the pan – its motion will stir the milk and prevent scalding.

Prevent milk from spilling over

While boiling, remove pan from heat when you see the milk rising, and put it down with a good bump.

Stop an oven from smoking

If you open your oven during cooking, and smoke pours out, you have a spillage problem. That said, the show must go on – locate the spillage and cover thickly with salt. The smoke will abate, you can shut the oven, and clean up the spillage once dinner is cooked and the oven has cooled.

Save dishes to which too much salt has been added

- ▸ Add a couple of spoonfuls of milk.
- ▸ Put some slices of raw potato in the middle of the pot.
- ▸ Add a teaspoon of sugar.

Stop toast going soggy

Tap each slice all over with a teaspoon immediately it pops out of the toaster. Then place in rack.

Rid the smell of onion from knives

Take a carrot and run the knife blade through it two or three times.

Get your Yorkshire puddings right

The batter should be made with half water, half milk, and be mixed several hours in advance. Leave to stand at room temperature. Your tin should be heated while still empty – place in the oven and, once hot, add some fat and heat further until smoking. Now, and only now, should you pour in the batter.

Cut very fresh bread

Heat the bread knife in hot water and the bread will cut as smoothly as stale.

Stop pasta from sticking

Add a teaspoon of oil (preferably olive oil) to your boiling water before adding the pasta. Once pasta is cooked and drained, pour a little boiling water through it, and stir. Serve immediately.

Revive cheese and ham

Cheese gone hard is not necessarily past it. Don't waste it until you have tried the following: Soak a clean cloth in white wine and ring out well. Wrap around the cheese and leave for several hours. Your cheese will be softened. Now it is up to you to taste it. Dried-out slices of ham respond well to soaking in a small amount of milk for ten minutes.

Soup too fatty?

Soak up any excess oil or grease oil or grease with kitchen roll placed on the surface. Alternatively, drop a lettuce leaf into the pot.

Food stuck to the frying pan

Is a royal pain, and an unnecessary one. Heat the frying pan before you add your oil, and see the difference. This does not apply to non-stick pans. Obviously.

Prevent a grill pan from smoking

When grilling meat, place half a slice of stale bread in the bottom of the grill pan (underneath the meat on the rack). It will soak up the fat and ensure a smoke- and fire-free experience.

Home-made stock gone cloudy?

Make it clear by adding a few empty eggshells and simmer for ten minutes.

Stale cereal

Will become crisp again when heated in an oven or grilled gently for several minutes.

A smelly fridge

Can be neutralised with a small bowl of charcoal or bicarbonate of soda placed on the middle shelf. Never

clean a fridge with disinfectant, as it will flavour food
for months to come. Rather, use a teaspoon of
bicarbonate of soda in warm water, rinse, and dry with a
clean cloth.

Soups and stews

Should be placed in freezer bags, then in boxes, before
going in the freezer. Once frozen, the boxes can be
removed to leave stackable bags. A great space saver.

Frozen stock cubes

Are easier to crumble.

Leftover salad soup

Don't throw a leftover salad away, even if it has been
dressed. Liquidise with a tin of tomatoes, a few drops of
Tabasco and Worcestershire sauce and – *voilà!* – you
have a nutritious snack.

TOMATO KETCHUP

Shake oh shake the ketchup bottle,
First none will come, then a lot'll

Freeze leftover wine

Until required for cooking. If you are a stranger to
leftover wine, you're presumably enjoying life. Good for you.

Eggs

Eggs, boiled

If an egg cracks when boiling, quickly sprinkle a teaspoon of salt into the pan and the whites will not escape.

How to tell if your eggs are fresh

Fill a deep bowl with water, and place eggs gently at the bottom. If they rise to the surface, do not even consider using them. Air gets into stale eggs and this much air means they are off. If one end tips up, they need using up within a day or so. If they lie on their side they are nice and fresh. Another way to tell if your egg is past it is to crack it into a frying pan. A fresh egg will hold its form, while an old one will run everywhere.

Say goodbye to discoloured eggs

Once hard-boiled, plunge your eggs into cold water to ensure the insides don't turn a peculiar colour. To cut eggs without crumbling them, dip your knife in boiling water before cutting each slice.

Poaching eggs is easy when you know how

Add a teaspoon of vinegar and a pinch of salt to a pan of water and bring to the boil. Remove from the heat. Use a spoon to swirl the water round, and break the egg into the middle of the swirling water. Cover pan tightly with a lid and leave for approximately two minutes.

For super-fluffy omelettes

Throw in quarter of a teaspoon of cornflour per egg – the difference is very noticeable. Works for scrambled eggs too.

CONTAIN A POACHED EGG

Cut both ends off a small clean can (e.g. tuna) and place in the water. Crack your egg into the can – genius!

Stop an omelette sticking

With a sprinkle of salt in the pan. Heat the salt for ten seconds before pouring in your beaten eggs.

Scrambled eggs sticking to saucepan

Will stick less stubbornly to the saucepan if you melt the butter in the pan before you add the egg. Also, remove from heat when eggs are three-quarters cooked. Cover and allow to finish cooking in their own heat. Your eggs will come away more easily and less elbow grease will be required when cleaning the pan.

Improve scrambled eggs

With a tablespoon of breadcrumbs, added before cooking, for improved taste and quantity.

Dirty scrambled egg pan

Fill with water and a couple of spoonfuls of dishwasher powder (crumbled dishwasher tablets are fine, too). Leave for half an hour and cleaning will be a doddle.

Vinegar stops eggs from cracking

Add two tablespoons to the water when boiling eggs. This will stop them cracking and make them easier to peel once cooked.

A sharp tap on the head with a spoon

Will make sure a boiled egg doesn't cook itself any further once it's out of the water.

To separate the yolk from the white

Break egg into saucer, place a small wine glass or eggcup (both upturned!) over the yolk, and pour off the white.

Dairy

Make butter go further

When making many rounds of sandwiches, stir in a little warm milk. This will soften it and make it easier to spread.

Milk, boiling

When boiling milk for hot chocolate etc, rinse out the saucepan with water beforehand, then add the milk. This stops the milk from burning and sticking to the bottom of the pan. If milk is about to boil over, remove from heat and give the bottom of the pan a short, hard knock on the surface you put it down on.

How to beat your cream better

Before whipping cream, chill the bowl and the whisk in the freezer for half an hour. Cold whipping equipment will beat your cream more efficiently. To reduce the chances of overbeating, make sure you add any sugar before beating, not afterwards.

Cream on the turn?

Add a pinch of baking soda to eradicate bad taste and halt the curdling process.

For fresh milk without a fridge
> Pour milk into a screw-top glass bottle and wrap in a blanket. Fasten blanket well, then plunge into cold water. Hang your swaddled milk in a cool, shady place outside, or keep in a cool cupboard or pantry. The milk will stay cold for as long as the blanket does.

Fish, Poultry and Meat

HOW TO COOK THE PERFECT STEAK

The key to cooking perfect steak is to rest it once you have cooked it – this allows the meat to warm through and tenderise itself. The authors have used this method time and time again, with great results. Cook a one-inch-thick steak as follows: Bring steak to room temperature before cooking. When ready, heat your pan over a high heat so it is hot, but not smoking. Brush your steaks with oil, or pour a little oil into the pan. (Use oil with a high burn point, such as groundnut or rapeseed.) Place your steaks in the pan – they should sizzle as they hit the heat. Cook steak without touching for the times below, then flip and, once again, do not touch. Once done, rest steaks on a plate and seal with foil.

Cooking times for a one-inch-thick steak:

Rare: One to two minutes per side – rest for six to eight minutes.

Medium rare: Two to two and a half minutes per side – rest for five minutes.

Medium: Three minutes per side – rest for four minutes.

Well done: four and a half minutes per side – rest for one minute.

Thaw fish in milk

Frozen fish should be defrosted in milk. This will give it a much fresher taste.

Marinate meat in a bag

Place meat and marinade in a sealable bag – when you need to turn meat over, just flip the bag. This trick also allows you to massage the marinade into the meat.

Over-salty anchovies

Should be soaked in milk for at least an hour before use.

The smell of kippers

Can be minimised if you wrap them up in foil and bake in the oven. Boiling them in water works too, but be sure to put a lid on the pan.

Hands stink of fish?

A good wash with toothpaste will put things right.

How to pluck a chicken

Soak bird in boiling water for one minute first. This makes plucking easier and stops feathers flying everywhere. Work from the breast towards the head, removing up to three feathers at a time. Be sure to give a sharp tug in the opposite direction from that in which the feathers point. Now move to the back, and finally the wings. Any small feathers and hairs should be burnt off with a taper. Wipe clean with a wet cloth.

Fry fish with peanut butter

Half a teaspoon of peanut butter at the side of the pan will help prevent the smell of fried fish spreading around your kitchen and further afield.

For a juicier chicken

Try stuffing a whole apple inside before roasting as usual. Discard apple before serving.

Tins of Spam in the fridge

Will slice better. As will other tinned meats.

For healthier bacon in the microwave

Place two pieces of kitchen roll on a plate, add a few

rashers of bacon, and cover with two more pieces of
kitchen roll. Cook on high – your bacon will go crispy but
the kitchen roll will absorb much of the fat.

Avoid splitting sausages

Cover your bangers with cold water in a saucepan, bring
to the boil and drain before grilling or frying.

Drop ice cubes into your soup

To skim the fat off while still in the pot. The fat will cling
to the cubes. Be sure to scoop them out before they
melt.

Bacon too salty?

Soak rashers in warm water for twenty minutes. Dab dry
with kitchen roll. Don't take a heavily salted bacon joint
anywhere near the cooker unless you have soaked it in
water overnight. If boiling bacon, a peeled potato in the
water will help remove salt.

Save your bacon . . . rinds

And use the fat for frying. Cook over a low heat in a
frying pan and strain the fat from them. This is perfect for
everyday frying and will keep in the fridge for a couple of
weeks.

For healthier bacon

Wash rashers under cold water for a few seconds, and pat dry with a kitchen towel. Place bacon in an enamel or earthenware dish, and cook in the oven. There's no need to add any oil or fat.

When tenderising your meat

Add a few drops of water to your beater and chopping board. This prevents the meat sticking.

Tenderise your meat in tea

A cheaper cut of meat (or an expensive cut that happens to be tough!) can be tenderised with tea. Marinate or cook in your favourite brew (no milk required).

Oysters in soda water

Soaking oysters in soda water will make their shells much easier to open.

Grab your bird

Don't faff around with utensils when removing a chicken or turkey from the roasting pan. Simply don some Marigolds, and lift your bird out cleanly.

For perfect crackling

Ensure the skin of your joint is dry before cooking, and rub in a small quantity of salt. There's no need to cover it in oil or fat, but do use a shallow roasting tin to guarantee maximum heat exposure in the oven. For super crispy crackling, wait until ten minutes before your joint is due out of the oven, then pour the juice of a lemon and the same amount of boiling water over the crackling. Turn the oven up to 230 degrees and cook for remaining time.

For juicier cold boiled ham

Let it cool in the water, rather than on a plate, before eating.

Lamb servings

Should always be on very hot plates. That way, any fat will not congeal.

Ditch your roasting rack

And place your meat on a layer of chopped onions, carrots and celery. The meat will cook just as well, and you'll be able to mash the vegetables into the meat juices to boost the richness of your gravy.

A good stuffing

Can be achieved with fewer eggs. Simply soak your
breadcrumbs in water before adding to the mixture, and it
will bind just as well.

When coating meat in flour

Shake the meat and flour in a paper bag. You'll make far
less mess, and save on washing-up, too.

Strong-smelling meat

Should not be discarded until you have washed it in cold
water and vinegar. If the smell disappears, your meat is
fine. If it persists, move towards the bin. . . .

Freeze your stock in ice trays

Then store as cubes in bags.

Kipper tips

To reduce oiliness, but not moisture, soak kippers in hot
water for a minute before cooling. Dry or over-smoked
kippers can be soaked for up to an hour to improve
flavour and plumpness. Dry with kitchen roll before
cooking.

Fruit and Veg

To double the juice from oranges and lemons

Heat them before you squeeze them. This can be done in the microwave, or by popping them in boiling water for five minutes.

Hot beetroots, how to peel

Immerse them in cold water and the skin will slide off easily.

Baked potatoes in half the time

A metal skewer or the blade of a stainless steel knife through a potato end to end will conduct the oven's heat and give you great baked potatoes twice as quick. They'll be doubly nice if you rub with olive oil and salt before cooking.

Store onions in old tights

Keep onions fresh, dry and in one place by keeping them in a stocking leg.

Cook potatoes quicker when running late

Before boiling, cut your spuds lengthways rather than across. They will be ready much sooner.

Keep watercress fresh

Keep in water, stems to the sky.

For marvellous mash

Substitute sour cream for milk. Warm the cream first, and add some grated nutmeg. Don't forget to add a knob of butter and, remember, the smaller you cut your potatoes, the quicker they will cook.

To keep mash warm

Heat some milk and pour a layer on top of mash. Keep pan in a warm place and the potatoes will stay heated and moist.

Easy-scrape new potatoes

Soak them for five minutes in hot water with a little bicarbonate of soda, then use a wire pan scrubber.

Scraped new potatoes will not discolour

If kept in water with a few tablespoons of milk added. They will remain perfect for several hours.

SOUP IS FREE!

Pick a good-sized bunch of nettle tops (making sure you're wearing rubber gloves). Wash four times over and remove all stalks. Bring a pan of water to the boil and cook leaves for ten minutes. Delicious served with butter.

Unbroken walnut kernels are achievable!

Soak for twelve hours in salty water before you bring out the nutcrackers.

Bananas in the fridge

Will darken but remain firm on the inside. Once sliced, stop bananas going brown by sprinkling them with lemon juice. This works for other fruits that brown easily.

Slice mushrooms quickly

An egg slicer works wonderfully for even and quick sliced mushrooms.

A pinch of sugar

Should be added when cooking carrots and turnips. It helps to bring out their sweetness.

The secret to shelling Brazil nuts

Place your nuts in a pan of cold water and bring to the boil. After one minute, plunge nuts into cold water. Once drained, leave to dry somewhere warm and get cracking.

Cut rhubarb with scissors

This saves time and leaves the skin intact.

Keep lemons in water

Lemons stored in a bowl of water in a cool, dark place
will stay fresh and juicy for longer.

Parsley-chopping cheat

Freeze fresh parsley in a plastic bag. That way, you can
crumble it, instead of having to chop.

Don't waste lemons

If you only need a little lemon juice, don't bother cutting a
lemon – the rest will only go dry. Instead, pop it in a bowl
of boiling water for a couple of minutes. Once heated
through, pierce lemon skin with a skewer or fork and
squeeze out required juice. Wrap lemon in tin foil and it
will keep in the fridge for several days.

Rind-grating tip

Before grating citrus fruits, dip the grater in cold
water. This will ensure the peel does not stick to the
grater.

The smell of cauliflower boiling

Is not one of life's pleasures. Add a bay leaf or lemon juice to the water and your nostrils will thank you.

Onion and Garlic tips

Never cry again

Tear-free onion chopping is possible. Either peel and chop under water, or (much more sensibly) wear a pair of goggles. Swimming goggles work particularly well. Alternatively, hold a fork or spoon between clenched teeth.

No more sticking

A sprinkle of salt on a garlic clove will prevent it sticking to knives, chopping boards or presses.

Onion first, garlic later

Onion requires longer cooking time than garlic, so when frying, add onion first and cook until transparent before adding garlic to the pan.

Stop fried onions from 'catching'

Avoid burnt onions by adding a pinch of salt to the pan when cooking.

Crushed garlic without a press

Add a pinch of salt and crush under the side of a knife
blade. The salt extracts the juices and helps form a paste.

Half-used onions

Will keep for longer if refrigerated in screw-top jars.
Same applies to peppers.

Strawberry hulling

Should be performed after washing, not before (unless you
like them soft and mushy, of course . . .)

Lettuce in your spin dryer

To dry a large amount of lettuce (or even a small
portion!), place in a pillowcase and give a spin (on cool!)
for ten seconds. Repeat until dry.

Peeled apples gone brown?

Avoid this unfortunate predicament in future by placing
them into some water with a little lemon juice. This
will keep them from discolouring for around ten
minutes.

For super-crispy celery

Stand your stalks in ice-cold water for half an hour, then serve.

Keep celery leaves

To make your own celery flakes, cut and wash leaves from celery stalks and place on a baking tray in a low oven. Wait until leaves are bone dry, then crumble and store in an airtight jar. Celery flakes are very handy when you need a tablespoon or two of celery, or if your fresh celery has wilted. A tablespoon will provide the flavour of a small stalk, and can be added directly to soups and stocks. For other dishes, rehydrate flakes before use – five minutes in three times their amount of water will do it.

Tomato peeling

Is infinitely easier if you cover the tomatoes in boiling water for a couple of minutes. The skin will come off effortlessly.

A knife and a lettuce don't mix

Tear lettuce, don't cut it. A knife will cause the leaf edges to turn an unpalatable brown.

Slugs and soil

Don't taste good. When washing lettuce, add a few
drops of lemon to the water to ensure swift departure of
any gastronomic nasties and leave the leaves nice and
crispy.

Old carrots

Deserve a new lease of life. Rejuvenate them and improve
flavour by adding sugar and butter after cooking in just
enough lightly salted water to cover them.

Save the vinaigrette till last

Don't toss your salad in vinaigrette or balsamic (or any
other vinegary concoction) until just before you serve it. If
left sitting, vinegar acid will collapse lettuce and turn your
tomatoes 'funny'.

Mint hint

When making mint sauce, chop the mint leaves with the
sugar to make the job easier.

To peel a pepper

Char the skin over a gas hob, and your job will be so much
easier.

For better-tasting strawbs

Juice an orange and pour over your strawberries half an hour before consumption.

Vegetable boiling rule

When cooking vegetables, always add them to boiling water rather than bringing the water to the boil with the vegetables.

For delicious cooked spinach

Just before serving, mix in a dollop of single cream, a pinch of salt, and grated nutmeg and black pepper.

Veg too soggy?

If you've overcooked your vegetables and can't serve them whole, don't get your knickers in a twist. Mash them (the vegetables, not your knickers) into a purée and heat in a pan until most of the moisture has gone. Stir in a knob of butter, sprinkle with sesame seeds and – *voilà!* – you've saved the day.

From the Pantry

Put a potato in your bread bin

To keep your bread fresh. Wash and dry your potato beforehand.

Wash your bread

A two day old loaf will benefit hugely from a quick rinse of its top and bottom under a cold tap before placing on a baking tray in a hot oven for a few minutes. It will come out tasting as fresh as the day it was baked.

Marshmallows gone hard?

Stale and hard marshmallows need not be disposed of. Put them in a bag with two slices of fresh bread and, two days later, all will be well . . .

Herb ratio

Dried herbs are much stronger tasting than fresh. One teaspoon dried herbs is the equivalent of two teaspoons of freshly chopped.

Out of coffee filters?

Fold a sheet of kitchen roll in two and you have an excellent temporary measure.

Brilliant golden breadcrumbs

Grate your stale bread, fry in butter till crunchy, and drain
on kitchen roll. Keep them in an airtight container for as
long as a month.

Crushed cornflakes

Are an excellent substitute for breadcrumbs needed for
deep-frying, crumbles and tarts.

Grill the bottom of a crumpet first

The top will be hotter; all the better to melt that butter with.

Heat tea leaves in the oven

For a few minutes before making your brew. The flavour
will be fuller and the leaves will go further.

For perfect rice

Bring the following to the boil: one cup rice, two cups
(minus one tablespoon) boiling water, one level teaspoon
salt. Simmer for ten minutes and, keeping lid on, remove
from heat. Do not lift lid or stir. Keep in a warm area for a
further ten minutes, and your rice should be ready, with all
water absorbed. Use a fork to fluff the rice, and if it is still
moist place a tea towel across the pan, replace the lid and
leave for a few more minutes.

Cook rice with lemon juice

Add a little lemon juice to the water to whiten the rice and separate the grains.

How to reheat rice

It's safe to reheat rice the following day (but not the day after). The best method is to put an ice cube on top of rice and pop in the microwave – the water from the ice is just enough to liven up the rice.

Don't discard jam and marmalade

Don't throw away jam just because it has gone hard and sugary. Place the jar in an oven or microwave for a short time. The sugar will melt and your preserve will be as good as new.

Beer in pancakes

A dash of beer in your pancake batter will give them a wonderful lightness.

Mustard rules

Never mix mustard powder with hot water (the colder the better) and always allow to stand for ten minutes before serving. This gives the flavour time to come out fully.

Don't double the salt
When doubling a recipe. Use one-and-a-half times the
original amount.

Dried tarragon soaked in water
Will have a much fuller flavour. Soak for ten minutes.

Recycle vanilla pods
They can be used time and time again. Extract from
sweet dishes, allow to dry and keep in an airtight
container.

New life for stale buns and scones
Dip in milk and heat them in a low oven for that
fresh-baked feeling.

DON'T RUN OUT OF STEAM
A marble in the steaming pan will rattle around,
alerting you to a pan that has boiled dry.

Oil in pasta water
A tablespoon of olive oil in your salted water will ensure
your pasta doesn't stick together.

Spaghetti test

If it's cooked, spaghetti will stick when thrown at a wall. Use one piece for this test – flinging the whole pan is not necessary.

Quicker jelly

Only use a small amount of hot water to melt the cubes. The rest can be made up with cold water and ice cubes. To guarantee your Jelly turns out easily, the mould should be wetted before the mixture is poured in.

Brilliant baking

Flour in your stockings

Fill the leg of a clean pair of tights with flour and store in an airtight container. Whenever you need to dust a pan or a board with flour, simply shake the leg for a fine covering.

A polythene bag by your side

Is handy when baking, especially when making pastry and kneading bread. Simply place your hand inside the bag whenever you need to pick something up, open the fridge or answer the phone, and avoid unnecessary mess.

Keep your nuts in place

To stop nuts or dried fruit sinking through the mixture to the bottom of the cake tin, try coating them in flour before you mix them in.

Floss your biscuits

If your biscuits or cookies are stuck to the baking tray, slide a piece of dental floss underneath them. Make sure it's not the mint-flavoured sort.

A bowl of water in the oven

While cooking a fruitcake will help to keep it moist.

Biscuit cutting

Instead of using rings, try rolling your dough into a long sausage shape, then slicing.

Don't waste chocolate

Grease your bowl with butter before melting chocolate. This prevents unnecessary sticking.

Pie identifier

When you bake pies, score a letter in the pastry (B for beef and so on) before freezing.

Avoid burnt piecrust edges

When baking, place strips of aluminium foil over the edges of pies. This will prevent them from burning and leave them golden brown.

Save butter wrappers

Freeze margarine and butter wrappers, and pull them out whenever you need to grease a baking sheet or pan.

Hard brown sugar

Can be grated if you are running short on time, or can't be bothered to soften it.

Cold butter from the fridge

Can be grated into a warm bowl to prepare it for creaming.

When measuring treacle or syrup

Dip measuring spoon in boiling water before use – treacle and syrup will turn out quicker.

Keep squeezy bottles

Ketchup and relish bottles can be washed and filled with icing for precision cake decorating.

Economise on scales

Save time by bearing in mind that one ounce (twenty-five grams) of flour or sugar is a heaped teaspoon or a level tablespoon respectively.

Not all sponges are born equal

But you can make sure two halves of a sponge sandwich rise evenly. Simply place them on the same oven shelf.

Fed up with sticky beaters?

Prevent butter from sticking to your beaters by placing them in hot water for five minutes before use.

Cut a delicate or spongy cake

With dental floss for a good clean cut.

White beating made easy

Make sure your eggs have been out of the fridge for at least an hour before you need to beat them. Add a pinch of salt to the whites, and beat with a whisk in a clean bowl.

For lighter scones

Replace milk in the recipe with yoghurt.

Accurate treacle measuring

Place the tin in a warm oven for five minutes. The heat will make it go runny and it will be easier to measure.

Unwanted egg yolks

Needn't be thrown away. Drop them in a bowl of cold water and keep in the fridge for up to three days.

Is your cake cooked?

The best way to check is to insert a skewer into the middle of the cake. If it comes out cleanly and easily, the cake is ready.

For a moister Christmas cake

Leave the mixture in the tin for a day before you bake it.

An elastic band on your mixing spoon

Will prevent it sliding into the mess in a mixing bowl. Wrap a band around the top of the handle and your spoon should rest easy.

Cake tins in water

To remove a cake easily from a tin, dip the tin (with cake inside) in a sink of hot water. After a few seconds, the cake will turn out nicely. Alternatively, place tin on a damp tea towel and count to ten before turning cake out.

Store cake with bread

Cake will stay moist if you keep a couple of slices of bread beside it in the tin.

Measure dry ingredients first

Use the same utensils to measure dry ingredients before wet, and you will save yourself time and washing-up.

Help!
Averting disaster in the kitchen

Save a burnt stew

By not stirring it. If you suspect whatever is at the bottom of your pan has cremated, pour contents into another pan. The burnt bits will not come along for the ride, and you may have averted complete disaster. You may need to add a bit more water, stock or seasoning to your rescued dish – much better than going back to the chopping board.

Keep a custard from curdling

Add a teaspoon of cornflour to egg custard.

Run out of cooking chocolate for baking?

A teaspoon of butter and four tablespoons of cocoa are a great substitute. Or tell your partner to remove their feet from the coffee table and get down the shops. . . .

Cream drought

A great single cream alternative is four ounces (125 grams) of unsalted butter melted into quarter of a pint (150 millilitres) of milk. Heat without boiling and stick the mixture in a liquidiser for ten seconds.

Burning butter

Can be avoided with a spoonful of oil in your pan.

Stubborn lumps in your sauce

Are best removed by straining through a sieve.

Save rancid butter

By placing it in a bowl and leaving until it reaches room temperature. Mix well with two tablespoons of milk, and pour off any excess. The rancid flavour will be gone.

'Dear me, I've run out of self-raising flour'

Never fear, it's easy to make. Simply add two and a half teaspoons of baking powder to eight ounces (225 grams) of plain flour. Mix well, and you're done.

Fruit cake gone dry?

Don't despair. Simply take a skewer, make several holes in the top of the cake and add a couple of teaspoons of brandy.

Clean up flour and dough with salt

Sprinkle salt over baking-day surfaces. A quick wipe with a sponge will clean everything away.

Kitchen Garden

Grow your own herbs

Constantly purchasing herbs from the supermarket is a costly affair. Here's how to ensure a cheap and ready supply is always at your fingertips. As a general rule, sow seeds in spring, and be sure to mix in a little sharp sand, as it keeps the moisture in and the slugs at bay.

Basil

There's no reason why a pot of basil from the supermarket, or from seeds, can't last a whole season. Sweet basil (*ocimum basilicum*) has larger leaves than bush basil, so use the sweet variety where possible. Prune top shoots regularly to ensure maximum bushiness, and get rid of any white flowers. Keep your plant by a sunny windowsill and, if planting outdoors, do so in May, once the winter frosts are a distant memory.

Chives

Chives will thrive in pots kept indoors, but they have a big appetite for the nutrients found in soil, so make sure you use a good fertiliser.

Coriander

Plant some crushed coriander seeds in spring, and in two weeks you'll have more than enough for a curry or two.

Dill

Should not be grown near fennel. They are relatives and we all know that cross-pollination is not a good idea.

HERBS FOR PEST CONTROL

If you grow your own fruit and veg, herbs can help you no end when it comes to keeping unwanted creatures at bay. Rosemary near beans will guard against weevils, marigolds will see off carrot fly, basil will put flies off potatoes, aphids don't like chives, and ants can't stand mint. Garlic prevents potatoes blighting and horseradish will see off any beetles.

Greenfly

Don't like mirrors – or so they say! Stand your pot on a mirror and see for yourself. Planting a clove of garlic in the soil will also keep greenfly at bay.

Plant-eating pests

Don't like garlic. To keep slugs and caterpillars away, use garlic spray. Mix three ounces (70 grams) of chopped garlic with two teaspoons of paraffin. Dissolve two teaspoons of soap into a pint (600 millilitres) of water and mix everything together. Store in a plastic container, and spray onto leaves when required, not forgetting to mix one part of your anti-pest potion with twenty parts of water.

Lolly sticks
Are great markers for seedlings. Save them up in the summer months!

Store bulbs in stockings
Or tights. Pack them in and hang them up so the air can circulate around them.

Food Storage

Avocados
Ripen slower in the fridge, and faster when buried in a bowl of flour.

Unripe fruit
Will ripen more quickly when placed in a bowl alongside bananas.

Apples help potatoes
Pop an apple in with your potatoes, and they won't grow buds nearly as quickly.

Chalky brie skin

Will benefit from being scraped by a fork. This allows it to breathe and become soft and delicious again.

Cakes

Should be stored in tin boxes, not plastic ones, as plastic is porous and you need an airtight seal. Avoid storing fruit cakes in foil for too long. The fruit's acid can corrode the foil, which leads to mouldy cake.

Keep biscuits crispy

Simply keep a sugar cube in your tin.

Cream

Will keep for longer if you store cartons and tubs upside down.

To keep cheese fresh

Wrap it in greaseproof paper and pop it in a plastic bag. It is best kept at the bottom of the fridge. Hard cheese will stay fresher for even longer if the cut edge is covered in a thin layer of butter before wrapping.

Dried-up cheese

Should be grated and frozen for later use in sauces.

Grating cheese

Is made easier if you place it in your freezer for fifteen minutes beforehand. The colder the harder, and the easier to grate.

Freezing fish

A clean, empty fruit juice carton is a very handy place to freeze fish. Drop your catch in, top up with water and staple the carton shut.

Tomato purée left-overs

Will stay fresh in a small bowl if you cover the surface with olive oil and refrigerate.

Ripen fruit quicker

Underripe pears, peaches and tomatoes will improve if you place them in a brown paper bag alongside an apple. Pierce the bag a few times and leave overnight.

A lettuce in newspaper

Will keep for a few days if you leave it somewhere cool.

Melons in plastic bags

Do not absorb other food smells from the fridge.

Put an apple in your cake tin

To keep your cake moist.

Tissues and tomatoes

Go hand in hand. When storing tomatoes (or other green vegetables), a few tissues thrown in will absorb moisture and ensure your produce stays firm.

The best bread bins

Bread will stay moist the longest when stored in earthenware. When washing bread bins, use a dash or two of vinegar in a pint of water to guard against mould.

Knackered crackers

Are easily avoided. Keep your cream crackers fresh by wrapping them tightly in polythene and storing in the fridge.

Home is Where the Heart is

House Beautiful Hints

Put toothpaste on your walls

Screw and nail holes can be hidden with a spot of white toothpaste. Handy when moving picture frames around.

Light a match in the bathroom

To dispel nasty smells. Once lit, hold match upright for five seconds and blow out. Now take a deep breath, or leave the room. . . .

Snow will clean an Oriental rug

The best way to clean an Oriental rug is to lay it face down on virgin snow and then walk all over the back of the rug (if you don't have any snow handy, damp grass is a good alternative). Leave for two hours, beat the rug and then vacuum. This technique avoids the use of modern rug cleaners and liquids, which can damage delicate rugs.

Cling-film your wood

Polished wooden surfaces can be protected from watermarks and other stains. A layer of cling film is especially handy before parties.

Bad cooking odours

To instantly freshen and clear the air of cooking odours, add a few drops of lavender essential oil to a cup of boiling water. The air will be fresh immediately.

Wax your ashtrays

A dab of wax polish will make your ashtrays so much easier to wipe clean.

Piano keys

Dust the keys well, then dip a clean cloth in some methylated spirits so it is damp and wipe over the keys. The meths cleans well and dries almost instantly, so will not damage the keys at all. Alternatively, damp a cloth lightly in milk, then wipe over the keys. Polish immediately with a soft, dry cloth.

Coffee for your furniture

Nicks and scratches in furniture can be covered up with instant coffee. Make a paste with water, and rub in with a soft cloth. Better still, blend the paste with beeswax first.

Dust inside stringed instruments

Can diminish the quality of tone. Remedy this by throwing a handful of rice into violins, cellos, guitars etc. Shake gently and empty for dust-free music.

Dents in carpets

Can be removed by placing an ice cube or a tablespoon of cold water in the dent. The carpet will come back to life as the pile dries.

New carpets

Should be swept with a stiff broom, or wiped with a damp cloth for the first few weeks. This will prevent your vacuum cleaner from becoming clogged.

A lifeless carpet deserves a second chance

Mix boiling water and vinegar in three:one ratio. Once cool, use a well-wrung cloth to gently massage your carpet. Faded colours should come back to life. If they don't, perhaps it's time for a visit to the local tip.

Black heel marks on floors

Erase with a pencil eraser. Sliding-door tracks are easier to clean with the aid of an eraser, too. Wrap a thin, damp cloth around it first.

Rubber cap for a broom

Cut the finger off an old rubber glove and stretch one over the end of each of your broom handles. That way, they won't slide around when propped against walls, and you'll avoid scratches, too.

For stiff ruffles in curtains

Give curtains a light covering of hairspray to stop them from drooping.

For a makeshift bookend

Cut the hook off a wire coat hanger and bend the rest to a right angle. Slide one end underneath your books, and you're done.

Leave lemons in the house

Before you go on holiday, leave half a sliced lemon in each room. When you return, your house will smell as fresh as daisies. Or lemons.

Milk mends china plates

Small cracks will disappear if you place your plate in a pan full of milk, bring to the boil and simmer for fifty minutes.

For snug candleholders

Place rings of newspaper around the inside of candle-holders to ensure a tight fit.

China and paper plates

Layer delicate china plates with paper plates to ensure your china remains chip- and scratch-free.

Shampoo carpets with care

Too much water will oversoak the carpet, which may bring colour through from the back. Never scrub a carpet – think of it more like a massage. . . .

Scorched pile?

Slight scorching on a carpet can be dealt with by rubbing with the cut side of a raw onion.

Put damp covers on your furniture

Once cleaned, ensure your washable upholstery covers fit back on snugly by replacing them while a little damp. Don't be scared to iron them while on the furniture, but be sure to use a cooler setting when dealing with foam fillings!

Cologne in the vacuum cleaner

A piece of cotton wool soaked in cologne or fragranced oil and dropped into your vacuum bag will freshen the air wonderfully.

Candles

A candle will fit easier into a candlestick and remain stable if dipped first into very hot water. Freezing candles before use makes them last a lot longer.

Leather book bindings

Should be well looked after. To clean and rejuvenate them, beat equal amounts of milk and egg white and apply gently with a soft cloth. Leave for a few minutes, then polish with another cloth.

Mattress sense

When new, turn over and swing around spring mattresses once a week. This helps the filling settle in. After a month of this, turn your mattress quarterly. Use the seasons as a reminder: switch ends in spring by putting the foot where the head was; turn over in summer, leaving head at top; in autumn switch ends without turning over, and in winter just turn it over again.

Bust those dust mites

Never vacuum a spring mattress, as this can dislodge the filling and leave you with a lumpy place to sleep. Much better to clean with a stiff brush and collect dust into a dustpan.

A polish too far

Never polish floors on which you will place rugs or mats – a recipe for disaster. To stop a rug slipping, brush a few strips of latex adhesive across the back. Dry for a couple of hours before laying the rug down. Jampot washers sewn onto the corners of a small rug will hold it in place.

Banish musty smells from wooden wardrobes and chests

By placing a slice of white bread in a bowl, covering it in vinegar, and leaving the bowl inside closed furniture for a day or two.

Gravy or sauce on a tablecloth

If you are mid-meal, and your precious cloth cannot be removed and immediately soaked, worry not. A covering of talcum powder will help to absorb the mess until the meal is over.

An old toothbrush

Should not be discarded. Rather, boil in water to sterilise, and put aside until later for cleaning hard-to-get-to nooks and crannies. Think blenders, toasters, taps and graters. . . .

Make your own wood-polishing cloth

Mix an eggcup each of paraffin and vinegar in a screw-top jar. Stuff a clean duster into the jar, close the lid tightly and leave overnight. In the morning you will be the proud owner of a splendid polisher.

House Plants

Line your plant pots with tights

Old tights or stockings at the bottom of a pot keep the soil in while allowing the water to drain.

Castor oil for your plants

Add several drops of castor oil to the soil of your house plants every six weeks to make them healthier and greener.

Talk to your plants

It may sound crazy but there is good evidence that talking to and stroking your plants makes them grow

better and remain healthy. Why not put this to the test by
taking two of the same plant and spoiling one, but not the
other. . . .

Baste your plants!

Hard-to-reach containers, tiny pots and mini plants can
be easily watered using a baster. The extra control and
shape of the vessel makes accidents and spills less likely.

Ice cubes in hanging baskets

Are a good way to water them without water dripping all
over the place.

Don'ts for plants

Don't place plants in direct heat or in draughty places.
They need a cool and even temperature so don't put
them on the shelf above the radiator! Don't leave plants
right next to a window unless it is double glazed, or the
plant is in front of a curtain. The cold atmosphere will
ruin it.

To water or not?

A good test to establish if a plant is thirsty is to press a
piece of newspaper into the soil. If the paper dampens, the
plant does not need a drink.

How to handle a parched pot plant

Lower plant into a bucket of water until pot is
submerged, and if bubbles appear it means the soil has
dried out. Wait until the bubbling stops before removing
the pot.

While you're on holiday

Put a couple of old towels in your bath and soak them
with water. Place your pot plants on the towels, and they
will soak up the water gradually while you get sunburn.
Or go one step further and make a greenhouse in your
bath. Fill it with fifteen centimetres of water and put
plants in, being sure to keep them above water level.
A few upturned buckets will come in handy as plant
stands. Tape a sheet of polythene to the wall and hang it
over the edges of the bath. The damp atmosphere
will ensure your plants stay well for a good couple of
weeks.

Stop watering house plants

As soon as water runs out from the pot's bottom. Leave
plants to stand in excess water for fifteen minutes, then
pour it away.

Window boxes

Layered with gravel will ensure the rain does not splash soil onto your windows.

FOR HAPPY HOUSE PLANTS

Feed plants with melted snow, as it is packed with minerals. They will also be delighted with flat soda water, water used to boil eggs, and water from defrosted fish.

Liven up china with Vaseline

Rub with Vaseline, leave for an hour, then polish. Your beloved china will be dull no more!

For stronger glassware

Fill your biggest pot with water and bring to a slow boil. Carefully add glassware and simmer gently for an hour. Your glass will be stronger for it.

Need to keep china steady for glueing?

Set your crockery in a bowl of slightly damp sand. If you are glueing a plate, hold joined pieces together with clothes pegs at the edge.

Sharpen needles with sandpaper

Poking a blunt needle through a piece of sandpaper several times will put the prick back in its point.

Velcro on your television

If you're tired of looking for your remote control, try this: attach a piece of sticky-backed Velcro to the side of your television, and tack the corresponding piece onto the back of your remote control. Keeping the remote in one place means you'll never look under the cushions again.

Don't hang a cherished painting over a fireplace

Smoke and soot will darken and damage a painting so, if you value it, hang it elsewhere.

For dust-free curtains

Sheer curtains will shun dust after a light starching.

Freeze your books

A musty-smelling book will come out fresh if left overnight in a frost-free freezer. This applies to many other items, including Tupperware (who knows, it may even work for shoes).

Seal slatted cupboards

Slatted cupboards look good, but they let in dust and moths. To remedy this without ruining the appearance, tape pieces of waxed paper to the inside of the doors.

Freshen your kitchen in minutes

Turn your oven to its highest setting and, leaving the oven door open, cook an unpeeled lemon for twenty minutes.

Sharpen a knife on a mug

The base of an unglazed mug will work as well as a whetstone for sharpening a knife. Hold it at a shallow angle and draw across. Repeat a few times, always moving in the same direction.

Keep hats and bags in shape

Give them a good stuffing with newspaper.

Hooks inside your wardrobe door

Are a handy place to hang up necklaces and other jewellery. It is also helpful to have items close to hand for matching with outfits.

Small spots on ceilings

You may be just as well covering these with a little white shoe polish, or paint. Nobody will notice, and you won't risk spreading the stain when attempting to clean it.

Rust on a countertop

A good scrub with lemon juice and salt should sort this out.

Mattress stains

Should disappear if rubbed with a thick paste formed of cornflour and water. Allow to dry for a few hours before vacuuming clean.

Clean crystal with a shaving brush

Lather up deeply etched crystal with a shaving brush. The bristles are perfect for cleaning hard-to-reach corners, but will not scratch.

Wax your windowsills

A layer of wax polish will make dirt and dust so much easier to remove in the future.

Don't go mad with the vacuum cleaner

Sometimes we vacuum when we need not vacuum at all, and this can cause unnecessary wear and tear on carpets. Out-of-the-way places should be cleaned just once a month, while high-traffic areas need attention once a week.

Tea on mirrors

Strong, cold tea makes an excellent mirror cleaner. Apply with a soft cloth and buff dry with scrunched-up newspaper.

Sticking drawers?

Rub a candle along the runners.

Save screw-top jars

And screw the lids to the underside of cupboard shelving. Once filled with sugar, dried fruit etc., the jars can be screwed in. A nifty bit of space-saving storage. Useful in workshops too.

Never scrimp on vacuum bags!

Vacuum cleaners require air to work efficiently. Reused bags will be clogged up, the air will not flow properly, and you will lose suction.

Clean venetian blinds

Are sometimes easier said than done. Until now. Soak a
cloth in methylated spirits, wrap around a spatula or
wooden spoon and wipe between the slats.

Roller blinds playing up?

If your blind won't stay down, the chances are it needs
lubricating. Remove it from the brackets, and hold
upright so you can see the spring mechanism. Spray with
aerosol lubricant and allow some time for it to run into
the works.

Straighten a bent candle

Place it in a polythene bag and run under a hot tap, or
immerse in very hot water. Once the candle has become
soft and malleable, gently roll on a flat surface until
straight.

To remove wax from a candlestick

Remove as much as possible by hand or with a knife, then
melt remaining wax with a hairdryer and wash off with
warm soapy water.

LOGICAL WINDOW-CLEANING TIP

When polishing your windows wipe one side on the
horizontal, and the other on the vertical. That way
you will be in no doubt which side the smears are on

Keep a Sunday newspaper together

With a paperclip over the central fold. You may wish to
iron it first (like they did in the old days) to stop the ink
coming off onto your hands. Once you've finished reading,
consider spreading a few sheets under your doormat to
catch any dust and dirt that gets through.

Umbrella drips

Are soaked up nicely by a circular piece of foam cut to fit
the bottom of an umbrella stand.

Squeaky floorboards

Can be silenced with a sprinkling of talcum powder
between the boards.

Dark hallways and rooms

Hang a good-sized mirror in a gilt frame to lighten a dingy
room or hallway.

Restore a gilt frame

Blend an egg white with a teaspoon of bicarbonate
of soda. Apply to frame with a pastry brush, wait a
couple of minutes, and wipe off using neat washing-up
liquid.

Avoid too much spray wax

On wooden furniture. The wax will form layers and
become streaky. Rather, dust frequently and polish with
beeswax every three months. Beeswax should be left for
thirty minutes before receiving a good buffing from a soft
duster.

Rub a Brazil nut on wooden furniture

To remove white marks. Rub in the direction of the grain,
then polish as usual.

Make your sofa wear evenly

Rotate and reposition cushions on a regular basis.

Cigar and cigarette smoke

A hairnet stuffed with straw and hung from the ceiling
will absorb cigarette smoke. To remove the unpleasant
odour of stale smoke from a room, burn a little coffee on
a shovel or other fireproof vessel and carry it through the

part of the house where cigars have been smoked. This will remove all lingering smells.

Hanging paintings

Paintings and pictures should be hung at eye level. Never hang oil paintings above a fire or source of heat, as this will cause the paint to crack. To prevent picture frames (or mirrors) marking the walls, apply corn rings to the back corners.

Potato on a painting

To clean an oil painting, squeeze the juice from a grated potato into a bowl. Using a soft cloth, apply with a gentle, circular movement. Rubbing a cut onion over the surface will work too.

Avoid lacklustre leather furniture

Leather dries out and cracks with too much sunlight and central heating. Prevent this by mixing two parts raw linseed oil to one part wine vinegar. Shake well and apply evenly to leather using a soft cloth. Polish with a rag. Or you can apply wax shoe polish instead.

Flowers and Vases

Don't cut flowers in the morning

Wait until dusk. Flowers cut in the evening contain more nutrients and consequently last longer. Immediately after cutting, stand in water right up to their necks and leave overnight.

Crush a rose stem

At the bottom (or split it), remove damaged petals and strip all thorns before putting roses in a vase. The same applies to other woody-stemmed flowers.

To revive cut flowers

Give stems a snip and place in boiling water for several seconds. Transfer to a vase and leave flowers up to their necks in water for two to three hours.

Keep cut flowers fresh for longer

Dissolving aspirin in their water will keep flowers perky, and a pinch of salt or small piece of charcoal will help the water stay fresh. Change water once a day and move flowers away from warm rooms at night.

Pennies for tulips

Add a few copper pennies to the vase water to stop tulips drooping.

Sugar for chrysanthemums

Add two teaspoons of sugar to the water to keep them fresher for longer. Sugar is also handy for marigolds – a teaspoon in their water will reduce the strong smell they give off.

Short-stemmed flowers

Will stay fresh twice as long if you put them in a bowl of well-watered sand.

Nasturtiums are loners

Never add a nasturtium to a flower arrangement – any other flower sharing the water will fade and die. Leave nasturtiums to themselves!

Don't buy flowers on a Monday

The chances are they will be left over from the weekend and less than fresh.

Singe poppy stems

With a candle or lighter before plunging in water.

Roses love lemonade

Place lacklustre cut roses in a vase of lemonade to give them a lift.

Flower holders

Can be fashioned from a raw potato. Use a skewer to make as many holes as required, then place inside a vase.

Never discard a leaky vase

Not until you've plugged the hole with a drop or two of candle wax and refilled the vase with water. . . .

Flowers for buttonholes

Should stand overnight in water and be singed at stem end when removed the next day.

Rub garlic on a vase

A hairline crack on a vase should be rubbed on the inside with a peeled clove of garlic. This should seal it back up again.

Dried flowers

Wait for a hot day to pick flowers you intend to dry – they will contain less water and therefore dry quicker and better.

For fresher air

Marinate a handful of eucalyptus leaves in two pints of white vinegar for two weeks. Leave bowls of the mixture around the house.

Newspapers

Can do more than keep you up to date on current affairs. Using a newspaper on windows will shine them better than anything else. Moths can't bear the smell of ink, so any clothes wrapped in print will be safe. An iron dustbin can be disinfected by burning a few papers inside it every week.

Paint Sense

- ▶ Paint with an onion by your side. An onion sliced in two and placed cut side to the heavens will banish nasty painting smells.

- ▶ Cover your door handles in foil or plastic film so you can use them with paint-flecked hands.

► To stop skin forming on gloss paint, pour a thin layer of white spirit on before closing the tin. Alternatively, close lid tight and store upside down.

► Drill a hole in your brush handle. This enables you to thread it onto a nail and suspend the brush in cleaning fluid without the bristles bending out of shape on the bottom of the pot.

► Wrap brushes in cling film when you stop for lunch so you don't have to clean them every time you have a break. This works overnight too.

► If you're painting with a roller, line your paint tray with tin foil before pouring paint in it. When you're done, dispose of the foil and you have a clean roller tray.

► Don't throw lumpy paint away until you've tried straining it through an old pair of tights.

► Cooking oil is much better than white spirit for hand cleaning. A teaspoonful is normally enough. Rub in well, and wipe off with a towel. Your hands will be clean and soft from the oil instead of dry and hard from white spirit.

Baskets will be stronger

After a wash with soap suds every so often.

Wallpaper hanging

Is made easier for beginners if the wall is pasted rather than the paper.

Blow-dry your mirror

Hold a hairdryer to a steamed-up bathroom mirror – much better than smearing it with a towel or your hands.

Steamed-up bathroom mirrors

Can be avoided. Before taking a bath or shower, use a clean cloth to rub a drop or two of shampoo onto your mirror.

Dirty teapot spout

Dip a cotton bud in neat household bleach and go to work. This will produce great results, even on the filthiest of spouts, but be sure to rinse very well before pouring out your next cuppa. Alternatively, pack spout with salt and leave overnight. Fill with boiling water in the morning, and pour out.

Sash windows

Should stop sticking if you rub a wax candle inside the window frame and along the window's sides. If the problem continues, paint or damp may be the issue. In both cases, strip back window, leave to dry and repaint.

Mirror Mirror on the Wall

Beauty and Grooming Tips

Egg on your face

Use full-fat mayonnaise straight out of the jar as a fantastic facial mask to combat dry skin. Apply liberally and wash off after twenty minutes.

Salt water for dry skin

Surely not? Surprisingly, it is good for dry skin. A cup of sea salt dissolved in your bath will yield most satisfactory results.

Make your own herbal conditioner

Mix a tablespoon each of almond oil, lanolin and glycerine with four drops of rosemary oil and heat gently in a pan. Once hot, remove from pan and beat an egg into the mixture. Massage into your hair, and rinse after ten minutes.

Coffee grounds as hand softener

Don't dispose of used coffee grounds until you have rubbed them over your hands. Regular application will exfoliate and buff leaving your hands silky smooth.

Shiny nose

Dab the nose with the following sugar-and-water solution. Dissolve one or two sugar lumps (or teaspoons of sugar) in a saucer allowing one teaspoon of boiling water per lump. Rub this syrup onto the nose with your finger, dab very gently with a tissue and allow to dry. Apply powder or make-up as usual.

For stronger nails

Add a tablespoon of vinegar and a pinch of boric acid to quarter of a pint (150 millilitres) of olive oil. Mix well in a bowl and soak your nails for fifteen minutes. Repeat two or three times a week before bedtime. Dry your hands afterwards, but do not wash them.

Dull complexion

For beautifully fine and clear skin and to revive the complexion, wash your face in warm buttermilk instead of soap and water.

An effective facial toner

The cooking water in which asparagus, white onions or lettuce have been boiled makes an excellent facial toner to tighten the pores, stimulate the glands and whiten the skin.

Nails a little yellow?

Rub slices of lemon over discoloured nails, and any parts of your feet that have acquired a funny colour.

Teeth whitener

To whiten the teeth, brush with a little freshly squeezed
lemon juice. Brush immediately afterwards with a normal
toothpaste and rinse thoroughly as the acid in the lemon
damages the enamel. (We also have it on good authority
that salt makes an excellent tooth cleaner – it hardens the
gums and whitens the teeth. Rinse well, and avoid
swallowing.)

When you've run out of toothpaste

Use bicarbonate of soda as a fantastic substitute.

Silky skin treats

Mix equal parts of rose water and glycerine for a
wonderfully supple body lotion. Apply at bedtime. Mix two
parts glycerine with one part lemon juice for a gentle
hand lotion.

Tingly peppermint body scrub

Combine two teaspoons of vegetable oil and four drops of
peppermint oil with four tablespoons of salt. Rub on in the
shower for an invigorating wash.

Sticky plaster stains on skin

Will come away with a little lemon juice or eucalyptus oil.

No-water hairwash

To freshen greasy hair, dust your hair with cornflour or baby powder, and then brush out.

Tired, swollen feet

For weary feet in hot weather, soak them at night in a bowl of hot salt-water solution. Ordinary table salt is fine, or use some Epsom salts if you can get hold of them at the chemist. After drying, sponge your feet with cool vinegar. The vinegar if used again in the morning also combats smelly feet.

Tired, irritated eyes

Bathe tired eyes in a very mild, warm, salt-water solution, or in weak tepid tea. Alternatively, apply lukewarm, used tea bags (camomile tea bags are particularly good) to the eyes before reclining.

To soothe swollen eyelids

Apply a slice of raw potato, once in the morning and again at night.

For softer, cleaner hands

Avoid washing hands in very hot water, as this makes them rough and hard. Always rinse your hands in cold water after washing them in warm. This closes your skin's pores and prevents dirt getting in, so your hands stay cleaner for longer.

Freshen oily skin

After washing your face, mist it with apple cider vinegar from a spray bottle.

Put a bracelet on without help

If your bracelet clasp makes it tricky to put on without another pair of hands, do not despair. Use a piece of tape (masking tape is good) to fix one end of the bracelet to your wrist. Now you can use your free hand to do the rest.

Take two inches off your hips

Instead of joining the local gym, consider giving this advice from the 1950s a try: *'Place the heels together, chest up, chin in, hips back. Take a long breath and bring the hands above the head slowly, then down to the floor without bending the knees. Repeat ten or twenty times, night and morning.'* If you already have gym membership, don't rush to cancel it.

Hot and cold foot bath

Fill two bowls – one with very hot water, the other with very cold – so that, when feet are put in, the water comes to just above the ankle. Place feet in hot bowl for three minutes, then transfer to cold water for a couple of seconds. Repeat several times – your feet will soon be hot and your body should tingle all over.

For smooth feet

Rub a few dabs of Vaseline into your heels every day.

For a rosy-cheeked entrance

'On entering a drawing-room, ladies just before they make their entrance and become objects of interest for the gentlemen and ladies gathered in the room should pinch their cheeks to produce the rosy glow so much admired.' Blusher is another option . . .

Freeze your make-up

Eyeliners, lip and eyebrow pencils will be easier to sharpen to a fine point if you give them a couple of hours in the freezer first.

Shave with hair conditioner

It's a fantastic stand-in when you've run out of shaving foam.

Sweaty palms before a meeting?

Clammy hands can be embarrassing, and worrying about
an impending handshake only makes you sweat more. Give
them a quick rub with some antiperspirant for a quick fix.

Refrigerate nail polish

It will last longer and go on smoother. And clean your
nails with vinegar before you apply polish – it will stay on
longer.

Sterilise your toothbrush

Boil your toothbrush every couple of weeks to get rid of
germs. Replace every three months, and always discard a
toothbrush after you have been ill.

Spotty?

Dab the affected area with lemon juice several times a
day.

Right out of your hair

Shampoo residue in hair equals dullness. For maximum
shine, add the following to your rinsing water: a
tablespoon of lemon juice for blondes and one of cider
vinegar for brunettes.

Highlights for brunettes

Mix a teaspoon each of allspice and cinnamon with half a teaspoon of cloves. Add to a cup of water and simmer in a pan for ten minutes. Allow to cool, then strain and rinse through hair at the end of wash.

Camomile for blondes

Camomile tea is a great rinsing aid after shampooing. Make up a half-pint (300 millilitres) using any of the following: two camomile tea bags, two teaspoons of dried flowers, or a good handful of fresh ones. Brew for up to fifteen minutes before use.

Green hair from swimming pools?

Blond hair can take on a green hue when exposed to chlorine. Regular swimmers will find a good rub with tomato juice before shampooing will neutralise the problem.

HAIR CONDITIONERS

To strengthen and add gloss to the hair, try the following age-old formulae, because you're worth it:

Egg conditioner

For long or weak hair. Beat the eggs of two yolks with a
little warm water; add a pinch of borax and a teaspoon
of glycerine. Apply to dry hair before washing. Leave for
ten minutes or so, rinse with cool water (hot water will
make scrambled eggs). Shampoo as normal.

Beer hair rinse

To add body and shine to the hair use a beer rinse once a
month. After shampooing, use a bottle of flat beer to rinse
your hair and work through with the fingers. Rinse the
hair well with lukewarm water.

Cider-vinegar rinse

A good treatment for dandruff, helps with greasy hair
conditions, and will also add highlights to brown hair. Fill
a large glass with equal parts of cider vinegar and warm
water. Use as the final rinse for your hair after
shampooing.

A tropical hair treat

Coconut oil works wonders on dull, dry and splitting hair.
Massage well into your scalp. Immerse a towel in very hot

water, then wring out and wrap around your head. Remove towel when it starts to cool, reheat and rewrap. Repeat this process for half an hour.

For shining hair

Melt the marrow of a bone of beef in a large saucepan. Blend quarter of a pint (150 millilitres) of warm rum in which a sprig of rosemary has been infused. Massage mixture lightly into the scalp, wrap your head in a towel and leave for two hours. Shampoo, and for that extra shine add a few drops of lemon juice or cider vinegar.

Hard nail polish

Add a dash or two of nail-polish remover to bottles of hard or sticky nail varnish. Shake the bottle and apply.

To freshen skin

An equal mix of witch hazel and rose water will liven the complexion when dabbed on clean skin.

Diamond Service – Jewellery care

A drop of gin
Or whisky will clean a diamond very nicely.

Dirty jewellery
Will respond well to toothpaste applied with a toothbrush.

Wear your pearls!
The more, the better, even if you wear them under your clothes and out of sight. Your skin's moisture is beneficial, and prevents the precious pearls from drying up.

Nail varnish too thick to use?
Stand the bottle in a shallow bowl of boiling water. To keep it runny, store in the fridge.

An empty lipstick
Makes a great container for hairgrips.

For a dry complexion
Mix several drops of lemon juice and olive oil with an egg yolk. Apply to a clean face, and leave for ten to fifteen minutes. Rinse off.

For a greasy complexion

Beat an egg white. Once stiff, fold in two tablespoons of
cornflour and apply the mixture to your face. Wait until it
feels dry (your face will feel tight), and wipe off carefully
with a damp cloth. Rinse.

DIY facial

For an invigorating and infinitely cheaper alternative to the
salon, brighten yourself up with this home-made treatment:
Add a teaspoon or two of menthol crystals to a bowl of
very hot water. Drape a towel over your head and hold your
face over the bowl. Take slow, deep breaths for as long as
you feel comfortable. The steam and menthol will unclog
your pores. When you are ready, cover your face in a clean,
dry flannel. Before your skin is totally dry, apply olive oil or
moisturising cream to face and neck.

Fruit on your face

Don't throw away overripe soft fruits, as they are perfect
for home-made face packs. Use berries on their own, or
mixed with natural yoghurt, and mix pears and peaches
with a little cream. Leave on face for half an hour, then
wash off with warm water.

Nourishing and natural face mask

Mix egg white with oatmeal and apply to face. This will close pores and moisten skin. Leave for twenty minutes and rinse off with lukewarm water.

Lemons on your elbows

Rest your elbows in the skins of two lemon halves, and make a gentle circling movement. After ten minutes you will have soft, white elbows.

Avocado skins

Once you have eaten the flesh of an avocado, rub the inside of the skins all over your face and neck for a wonderfully nourishing, natural skin boost. Leave residue on your face for half an hour, then rinse off with lukewarm water.

Help for hardened hands

Blend equal parts of soap flakes, olive oil and granulated sugar and beat until all flakes have dissolved. Rub thoroughly into hands and rinse off after a couple of minutes.

No more split nails

Lemon juice applied to nails is known to help prevent cracking and splitting. Paint it on three times a day. Alternatively, soak your fingertips in warm water mixed with a tablespoon of bicarbonate of soda.

Handcream for your head

Handcream is a great hairspray substitute when managing flyaway hair. Rub a small amount into the palms of your hands and apply lightly to hair. Now brush or comb through.

Mayonnaise conditioner

Say goodbye to split ends by massaging a tablespoon or two of home-made mayo into your hair, paying particular attention to the ends. Wrap head in a warm towel and leave for thirty minutes before rinsing well with cool water.

Vaseline removes mascara

In addition to being a very effective mascara remover, petroleum jelly leaves your eyelashes shiny and promotes growth. Apply a little Vaseline to eyelids and lashes every night.

Make-up remover substitute
Sunflower oil works perfectly well for both face and eye make-up.

Rehydrate your mascara
Mascara that appears dried up and useless can be rescued. Ensure container is watertight before leaving it in hot water for a few minutes.

Fix-a-lipstick
All is not lost if a lipstick snaps in half. The two ends can be melted over a candle and stuck back together. Reshape with your fingers, then leave in the fridge until hard again.

Coughs and Sneezes

Home Health Hints and Tips on Common Ailments

Blisters

Can be guarded against in advance. In the week before a
long walk or run, rub surgical spirit into the feet, allow to
dry and dust with talcum powder. Do this in the morning
and at night. While exercising, wear two pairs of thin
socks dusted with talcum powder.

Chilblains

To relieve painful, itchy chilblains, mix one teaspoon
mustard with two ounces (fifty grams) of lard to a
paste. Apply liberally to the chilblains before bedtime,
then put on some cotton socks. Alternatively boil up
some celery and bathe chilblains in the cooled cooking
water.

Conjunctivitis and sticky eyes

For babies or children with gummy eyes and
conjunctivitis, prepare a camomile tea. When cool, soak a
clean cotton ball in the tea and use to gently clean the
eye. Use a new cotton ball for each wipe to avoid
reinfection.

Constipation

Sufferers should drink a glass of warm water last thing at
night, and again first thing in the morning. Eat plenty of

stewed fruits, figs, green vegetables and salads dressed
with plenty of olive oil.

Cold sores

At the first tingling hint of a cold sore, dab the area
with a clean cotton bud dipped in methylated spirits several
times a day. Many people swear by lemon juice, too.

For beautifully soft hands

Cover your hands with Vaseline, and don some cotton
gloves. Leave on overnight, and awake to a seemingly new
pair of hands!

Dandruff

Drink at least two litres of water every day, and try to
keep to a healthy diet with lots of salads, green vegetables
and fruit. Brush the hair regularly, and keep all combs and
brushes clean by washing every week. Try the following
simple home remedies if over-the-counter products have
failed:

▸ Mix two teaspoons of vinegar in six teaspoons of
water and rub onto the scalp at bedtime. Wrap a
towel round the head and leave on overnight. Wash
the hair the following morning with a mild baby

shampoo, then rinse again with a vinegar-and-water solution. Follow this routine once a week for at least three months.

▶ Make a tincture of thyme by boiling four to five tablespoons of dried thyme in two cups of water for ten minutes. Allow to cool, strain, and massage the tincture onto the scalp. Leave for half an hour before rinsing with warm water.

▶ Massage the scalp with almond oil, then wrap the head in a hot, damp towel. (Dip a towel in boiling water, wring out when cool enough to handle.) Repeat the hot-towel treatment three times, reheating as the towel gets cold.

Hiccups

Everyone knows a hiccup remedy – here are a few favourites:

▶ Eat a piece of dry bread and chew each bite slowly.

▶ Drink a glass of pineapple or orange juice.

▶ Place your finger firmly under your nose, as if you have a moustache, and press in hard for thirty seconds.

▶ Swallow a teaspoon of fresh onion juice.

- ► Add a teaspoon of apple cider vinegar to a glass of warm water and drink.

- ► Add a drop of peppermint essence to a sugar cube and suck.

- ► Mix two teaspoons of salt in a cup of plain yogurt and eat.

- ► Drink a glass of water from the far side of the glass, bending forward to do so.

- ► Gently inhale a little pepper – enough to make you sneeze a couple of times. Sneezing usually makes the hiccups disappear.

Insomnia

Add a few drops of lavender oil to your pillow. Also a warm bath before bedtime will raise your body temperature and prepare you for a good night's sleep. If you still cannot sleep, get up, drink a glass of milk and occupy yourself with something until you are tired. Worrying in bed will only worsen your sleeplessness.

Lost voice

Beat the yolk of an egg, then mix with the juice of a lemon, and enough caster sugar to sweeten. Eat in spoonfuls over a period of time to restore the voice.

Minor burns

If skin is unbroken, rub affected area with a slice of raw potato.

Splinters

To remove a painful splinter, fill a wide-necked glass bottle (a milk bottle is ideal) with hot water, then hold the part with the splinter over the neck and press down tightly. The suction acts as a poultice, bringing the flesh down, after which the splinter can be removed more easily.

Styes on the eye

Dip a regular (or camomile) tea bag in hot water. Allow to cool slightly then press against the closed eye. Leave for as long as you can. Repeat as often as possible, or better still, bandage the tea bag onto the eye and wear overnight.

Sunburn

▸ Cover the affected areas with a thick layer of natural full-cream yoghurt. Allow to dry. Rinse in tepid or cool water, and repeat as necessary.

▸ For sunburn on the face, slice a cold tomato from the fridge, lie down in a cool room and place the slices over the face.

▸ Mix water and bicarbonate of soda into a paste and apply to skin. Cover in a light dressing.

▶ Apply aloe vera gel, witch hazel or calamine lotion to the skin.

▶ A wet tea bag can also relieve stinging. Apply directly, or add several bags to your bathwater.

Swollen ankles

Rushing around all day can swell the ankles and exhaust the brain. Wrap your ankles in towels wrung out in very hot water. Lie down with your legs slightly elevated and covered with a light warm rug.

Indigestion

Sage leaves in boiling water, once cooled a little and swallowed (water only!), is very helpful when you've run out of Rennie. Alternatively, drink half a glass of water mixed with half a teaspoon of baking soda.

Salt water for a sore throat

Half a teaspoon of salt dissolved in a cup of hot water will make a sore-throat remedy to rival anything you can buy in the chemist. Gargle, but do not swallow.

Onions for faintness

If you suddenly feel faint or light-headed, waft a cut onion under your nose. This may well bring you back to your senses.

Soothe a wasp sting

    With apple cider vinegar.

Soothe a bee sting

    With toothpaste or a slice of cut onion wrapped to the
affected area.

Vinegar on a bruise

    Will lesson the swelling. Apply directly using cotton wool,
then bandage.

Banish biliousness

    Mix half a teaspoon bicarbonate of soda, the juice of one
lemon and four tablespoons of boiling water. Take small sips.

An ice cube on the tongue

    Will numb it and make the swallowing of bad-tasting
medicine much more bearable.

A mustard bath

    Is a Victorian remedy for cold symptoms. Such baths
produce heat and sweat which help to detoxify the body. A
mustard bath need not be too hot, since the mustard will
draw your blood to the surface of the skin, which generates
heat. Mix eight ounces of salt, three ounces of mustard
seed (crushed to a powder), and one teaspoon of grated

fresh ginger. Stir into a small cup of warm water with five drops of eucalyptus essential oil, and leave for twenty minutes. Draw a warm bath, add the mustard mixture and stir well. Soak for a minimum of fifteen minutes. Best before bedtime. (Not recommended for young children.)

For painless plaster removal

Take the pain out of peeling off sticky plasters – turn your hairdryer to a low heat, and soften the adhesive. Within seconds, the plaster will slide off painlessly.

Crush a pill

To crumble a pill quickly and easily, squeeze it between the bowls of two equally sized spoons.

Travel sickness

Can be helped with glucose tablets, which also raise your energy levels during long journeys.

Tired and shivery?

Add a handful of salt to a hot bath and have a good soak.

Home-made cough mixture

Blend equal measures of cod liver oil, runny honey and lemon juice. Make on day of consumption – a tablespoon

for adults and a teaspoon for children will calm a cough.
Take as and when required. A more old-fashioned
concoction is linseed oil, good rum and honey in equal
parts and taken in the same doses.

Vinegar for headaches

If you feel a headache coming on, dip a hanky in vinegar
and lay across forehead for several minutes. If your
headache is already well established, pop two cloves in a
cup of fresh tea and sip slowly.

Yoghurt helps diarrhoea

Yoghurt can kill the bacteria that often cause diarrhoea.
It should also be consumed when on a course of
antibiotics, which can kill off the good bacteria in the gut
which help keep us well.

Vinegar on itchy bites

Douse insect bites with vinegar on cotton wool for
surprisingly effective relief from itching.

Old socks in the freezer

Make fantastic compresses for headaches and bruises.
Make sure you wash them before freezing in a sealed
bag.

A tea bag on your gums

Will help stop the bleeding. Wet with cold water and apply
– handy for children who've just lost a tooth. Works well
for shaving cuts, too.

Tired feet?

Roll your bare foot over a tennis ball while watching TV.
The ball will give you a surprisingly good massage.

Athlete's foot

To relieve itching, soak feet in apple cider vinegar. Apply a
few drops of tea tree oil to the affected area. To prevent
reinfection, soak socks and tights in a solution of one cup
of vinegar to four cups of water, then wash as usual.

Motion sickness

Sucking on a lemon can offer relief from nauseous
feelings in cars or on boats.

Popcorn for injuries

Freeze unpopped popping corn in a sealable bag for use as
an emergency ice pack. Can be carried in a cool bag on
days out and to sporting events.

Oats soothe skin

Oats can help many a skin complaint from rashes to
sunburn and chickenpox. Fill the foot of a pair of tights

with oats, tie up and hold under the tap while you run a
bath. Hold onto your oaty tights, as they will make several
such baths.

Flour on cuts

A handful of flour on a cut can be useful to stop bleeding.
Wrap immediately in a bandage.

Heartburn

A pint of very cold water often helps, as will camomile tea
or sipping boiled water or lemon juice. Alternatively, down
half a dozen oysters. The choice is yours!

Tired, irritated eyes

Should be bathed in a solution of warm, salted water. If
you don't have an eyebath, an eggcup comes in handy.

Itchy eyes?

Dissolve a teaspoon of bicarbonate of soda into a pint of
water, and use this solution, rather than shop-bought
lotion, to bathe your eyes.

Toothache

Oil of cloves often works wonders, as does a pad of cotton
wool soaked in gin or whisky.

Aching joints

Massage aching joints with elder leaves for natural relief at the end of the day.

Hairdryers and chickenpox

A hairdryer on a cool setting can bring very welcome relief from the constant itchiness and misery of chickenpox.

Bleeding gums and ulcers

Swig a simple mouthwash of water with a few drops of vinegar.

Mosquito repellent on clothes

Will last longer than it does on skin, as your sweat won't wash it away so quickly.

Chapped hands

Vaseline and boracic powder, mixed in a two:one ratio, works marvellously.

Chapped lips

Add a few drops of rose water to a tablespoon of clear honey, and apply to lips regularly.

Salt for weak ankles

It is often said that weak ankles respond well to a rubbing with salt solution. One teaspoon of salt dissolved in a pint of water should be applied twice daily.

Bread on corns

For effective treatment of corns, soak a few slices of
bread in vinegar. Apply enough vinegary bread to cover
corn, and wrap with a bandage overnight. Repeat nightly,
and soak feet in hot water every three days, peeling off a
layer of corn during each soaking. Continue process until
the corn is history.

Lemon juice in the morning

Drink the juice of one lemon in warm water to improve
your complexion and add some sparkle to your eyes.
Lemons are packed with vitamin C and will naturally
cleanse you from inside to out.

Dry skin?

Mix 250 millilitres of rose water with a tablespoon of
runny honey for a wonderful skin balm. Alternatively,
for a ready-to-use cream, mix glycerine and rose water
in a ratio of two:one and store in bottle. Shake before
use.

Home-made mouthwash

Add a handful of lavender to boiling water, leave to cool,
then strain to make a cost-effective mouthwash.

Bad breath

Take your pick of the following, and chew: fresh parsley, coffee beans, cardamom seeds. Don't just brush teeth and gums – give the tongue a gentle brush at the same time or use a special tongue scraper. Gargling cider vinegar in warm water and sucking a slice of lemon can also help. If problem persists visit your dentist or GP.

Cucumber

Works wonders as an astringent for dull or greasy complexions. Peel, chop and mash one cucumber with two tablespoons of water. Leave for half an hour, then strain and refrigerate. Once cold, apply to skin and leave for a few minutes before wiping off.

Puffy eyes

Lie down for half an hour having covered your eyes with any of the following: cucumber slices, chilled tea bags, a bandage dipped in equal parts rose water and witch hazel (chilled well).

Rub a-dub-dub
Laundry and Clothes Care Hints

Surprise Coca-Cola tip

Instead of letting cola rot your teeth, why not save some and add it to your washing. It will work wonders on lingering grease stains.

Alternative to fabric softener

Just add two tablespoons of white vinegar to the main wash. Trust us.

A cup of coffee on your knickers

If black lingerie is somewhat faded and brown looking, throw a couple of cups of strong, instant coffee into the rinse cycle of your laundry. Works for other black cottons, too.

Favourite jumper shrunk?

Add some shampoo to lukewarm water and pop your jumper in for a soak. Once out of the water, attempt to reshape before drying flat on a towel. It might just work.

Material World

Yellowing nylon

Can be saved. Add three tablespoons of bleach and six tablespoons of dishwasher detergent to four litres of hot water. Allow to cool, then add your garments. Soak for half an hour, then rinse in cold water and a dash of white vinegar.

Lifeless silk

Can be rejuvenated with a few lumps of sugar added to the rinsing water after washing.

How to tell linen from cotton

Wet the tip of your finger and apply to material. If it's linen, moisture will show on the other side immediately. If it's cotton, this will take a little longer.

Woollen garments

Respond just as well to baby shampoo as they do to your regular detergent.

Winter woollens

All woollens and cashmeres should be hand washed in a mild hand-washing detergent or a baby shampoo and dried flat on a towel, outdoors in the shade if possible, before storing for the summer. Pack them in a clean cedar box or vacuum bag along with cedar wood balls or a sprig of lavender to further protect them from moths during the summer months.

The thinking person's guide to sock hanging

Peg your socks and smalls to coat hangers, then peg the hangers to the line. You'll save time outside, valuable line space, and yourself from getting too wet if you have to get the washing in from the rain.

Common sense in the airing cupboard

Stack your linen with the most recently laundered linen at the bottom of the pile to ensure everything is used in rotation.

Whites

To brighten a white wash, add a capful of ammonia to the detergent dispenser in the machine, or to the boiling water if washing on the stove. Take care and read label before using household ammonia.

White silk

To wash delicate white silk shirts, dissolve a little borax in a bowl of warm water and soak the garment in it for an hour. Then wash in clean warm water with a little mild hand-washing soap or white *savon de Marseille*. Never boil silk or wash in very hot water.

Quicker drying

Clothes will dry much quicker if your dryer is only half full. Don't forget to clear your tumble dryer of fluff after each cycle.

A stocking in your jumper

Will allow you to hang it out to dry and keep it in shape. Thread a stocking or pair of tights through the sleeves of a lightweight jumper and peg each end to the line.

Faded colours

Are often nothing more than a build-up of washing powder in fabric. Try rinsing faded items in warm water with a splash of white wine vinegar. This will displace any lingering soap and (fingers crossed) bring the colour back.

Faded black clothes

Are often not faded at all. Rather, a build-up of washing powder in the material creates an illusion of grey. Get back to black with a good soak in half a cup of vinegar diluted in a bowl of warm water.

Toilet water (eau de toilette)

Add a few drops of your favourite scent to the water in your iron. This will make your clothes and sheets smell gorgeous.

A stitch in time saves nine

Especially true before washing. Always mend damaged items before putting them in the machine. Being tossed around will only make tears and holes larger.

Steam clothes in the bathroom

Even if your clothes have been ironed, they may be a little creased and wrinkled after storage. For a quick fix, hang clothes up in the bathroom while you wash, and let the steam do the work for you.

Clean Velcro with a toothbrush

Velcro works so much better when it is lint free. A toothbrush is perfect for achieving this state of affairs.

For whiter hankies

Add a little cream of tartar to your wash.

Need to store old lace?

Place it between layers of waxed paper. This prevents rotting.

Dual-action pincushion

Turn a pad of steel wool into a cushion that sharpens pins:
cover it in fabric.

Tennis balls in your dryer

Will help to fluff up any down-filled items such as pillows
or jackets. Two or three will suffice.

Don't soak clothes in bleach overnight

Any stain removal or whitening will be done within
twenty minutes. Leaving items for longer will only
damage them.

For super-white whites

Follow this easy bleaching method. For cotton or linen,
mix a tablespoon of household chlorine bleach into eight
litres of cold water. Soak fabric for fifteen minutes, and
rinse before washing as usual.

A handy dryer

Strip the cover from an old sunshade or umbrella, and hang upside down on a hook in the ceiling, or from your washing line. A perfect way to hang up your smalls and save line space for bigger items.

Lace underwear and tights

Don't waste money on a net bag. Simply place delicate underwear in a pillowcase and wash as usual.

For fluffy towels

The trick is to soak your towels overnight in cold water with a cup of washing soda thrown in. Wash on the hottest wash the following day.

Zip up your flies

Close all zips, buttons and Velcro strips before washing. Open zips etc. can snag other garments in the machine.

A sticky zip

Can be made zippier by rubbing soap, a lead pencil or a candle on it. Zip it up and down a few times to keep the teeth lubricated.

Newly ironed clothes

Will crease easily. Wait a few hours before you wear or pack them.

Folding

Try to fold garments across rather than lengthwise. The creases will drop out more easily when you come to wear them.

For lint-free drying

A few decent-sized pieces of nylon netting in your clothes dryer will make lint a thing of the past.

Yellowing wool

Is easily whitened. Make a solution of cold water and hydrogen peroxide in a ratio of eight to one. Soak wool overnight (for up to twelve hours) before rinsing. Wash as usual.

Make your own starch

Combine a pint (600 millilitres) of water with fifty grams of powdered gum arabic. Cover and leave to set for twelve hours. Store in a well-sealed container.

Corduroy won't fade

As fast if you turn it inside out before washing. This reduces friction and helps prevent the pile from flattening.

Clothes pegs (wooden)

These will last longer from new if you boil them for ten minutes.

Stained feet of white socks

Add a couple of teaspoons of bicarbonate of soda to the wash.

Put your jumper in newspaper

Storing woollen garments in newspaper will keep the moths at bay during the summer months.

How to Make a Pomander

Pomanders look fantastic, smell fantastic and they help keep moths at bay. Save money by making one for yourself.

Take a small orange (a thin-skinned variety, if possible) and stud the surface with cloves. The

clove tips should be sharp enough to do this
without assistance. If not, use a pin or bodkin to
make holes – but be careful not to pierce the skin
to the point that the juice flows. Combine a
teaspoon of orris root with a teaspoon of cinnamon
(use cinammon alone if you have no orris root),
and roll the orange around in the powder (be sure
to rub as much of the powder in as you can). Wrap
well in greaseproof paper and place in a cool, dry
cupboard. After it has rested for six weeks, your
pomander is nearly ready to use. Unwrap, shake off
any excess powder, and place in your drawers and
cupboards, or hang from a ribbon in your
wardrobe.

For really clean tea towels

Add a scoop of detergent to a bowl of boiling water,
followed by the tea towels. Allow to soak until water is
cold, then rinse and dry.

Keep white linen out of the airing cupboard

Unless you have reason to turn it yellow . . .

Steamy velvet

Bring tired and scrunched-up velvet back to life by hanging in the bathroom while you run a bath. Relax while the steam works its magic.

Sensible sheet drying

Fold your sheets into four while wet, and peg to line with four pegs. The material will stay in shape and be a doddle to iron.

Use a matchstick

When sewing buttons. Buttons sewed too tightly will be useless. A matchstick placed between button and fabric will ensure an ideal gap. To make buttons stay on longer, paint thread with colourless nail varnish (after sewing, naturally).

Rejuvenate black clothes

Rub with a turpentine-soaked rag to remove shine from old black items.

Identify your sheets

While they're still folded. Avoid the hassle of folding the wrong-sized sheet back up by marking labels with a 'D' for double, a 'K' for king and so on.

Ironing in the Soul

When clothes are too dry

Items are so much easier to iron when slightly damp. If your clothes are too dry, place in the fridge for five minutes. For extra dampness, spray with water and place in a plastic bag. Tie up the bag and leave for a few hours – a great excuse to do something altogether more fun!

Iron your clothes from both sides

Place a sheet of aluminium foil under your ironing board cover to double the heat and halve the effort – the foil will reflect the heat up into your clothes.

To remove shine from trousers and skirts

A solution of warm weak ammonia solution (one teaspoon per pint (600 millilitres)) dabbed on before ironing should do it.

Corduroy

Should be ironed inside out through a slightly damp cloth.

Rainwater in your iron

Will ensure it doesn't clog up.

Hats the way to do it! Hat cleaning in a jiffy . . .

Felt hats

Combine white spirit and French chalk to make a paste. Rub gently into hat. Once paste is dry, brush off.

Straw hats

Place a cloth in soapy water, then squeeze out and wipe hat. Now add a teaspoon of salt to a tablespoon of lemon juice, and apply. Rinse in cold water and allow to dry naturally.

Silk hats

Use lukewarm water with a dash of baby shampoo, and rub gently with a soft cloth. Sponge clean with a little warm water and allow to dry naturally.

Dry a cloth hat on a balloon

To keep the shape of a cloth hat, place it on top of a balloon. Be sure to fix the balloon to a surface.

Fluff and hair

Can be collected from dark material using Sellotape wrapped around the fingers – sticky side out of course. Avoid dust on navy and black items by hanging them inside out.

Elastic bands on hangers

Will stop clothes slipping from them. Wrap a couple of bands around each shoulder.

Stockings in the freezer

Will last longer, as will tights. Rinse in warm water, wring out and pop in a plastic bag. Seal and leave to freeze overnight. Thaw before use . . .

Tights laddering

Dab a ladder with wet soap or clear nail varnish to stop it spreading. To help prevent tights from laddering, wash them in a weak soap solution, but do not rinse.

Treat lace well

Cover with clean white tissue paper before ironing. This prevents shininess developing. Soak tired lace in sour milk before washing.

How to fold a kilt

When packing a kilt (or any pleated skirt), roll up lengthways and place in the leg of a pair of tights. This prevents creases and keeps the pleats in place.

Black leather gloves

To refresh old black leather gloves, mix a few drops of black ink in a teaspoonful of olive oil. Apply with a soft brush, and leave to dry in the sun. They will look as good as new.

Muddy umbrella?

Give it a rub with a rag dipped in methylated spirits. This method is unsuitable for silk umbrellas, however. Such delicate specimens should be rinsed gently in a pint of hot water in which a tablespoon of sugar has been dissolved.

Dyeing

If you need to dye socks or stockings, add some darning wool to the dye. That way, you have the right-coloured wool for when the items need darning.

Can't zip up your dress?

Thread a shoelace through the zip tag and pull gently.

Shoes and Socks

Run out of shoe polish?

Olive oil is a great substitute. Rub onto shoes and buff as you would with regular polish.

Leather shoes too loose?

Wet their insides, and dry them outside in the sun. This should shrink them a little bit.

Shoes too tight?

Stuff with wet newspaper and leave overnight. For leather shoes only.

Dip frayed shoelaces in nail polish

To make them easier to thread. Leave to dry for ten minutes before reintroducing laces to shoes.

Toothpaste on white leather

White toothpaste works a treat on white leather shoes and trainers. It makes them smell minty too (but we're not sure how this is useful!). Rub on, then rinse and dry.

Drying leather shoes and boots

Boots and shoes should never be put away when they are wet, nor dried by the fire or near direct heat such as on a radiator (or in the oven!). Stuff them with newspaper and turn them on their sides in a cool, dry room.

Feed your leather

All leather needs regular nourishment. A good leather cream or dubbin should be rubbed in about once a month – only a little is necessary – then well rubbed in until the leather has absorbed it.

Keep shoes aired

Don't shut boots and shoes away in a closed cupboard as they need air if they are to wear well.

Alternate your shoes

Never wear the same pair of shoes or boots continuously – two or more pairs worn alternately will last far longer than if worn day after day.

Removing mud from leather boots and shoes

Remove mud stains with a woollen cloth and some Vaseline, stuff with newspaper and leave for a day. Polish and shine, and they will be as good as new.

Storing shoes

Ideally, store unworn shoes and boots on 'trees' to preserve the shape and the leather.

Stains on suede shoes

Use a soft cloth to rub a dash of white vinegar onto the stain. Allow to dry naturally, and brush the suede. For a general freshen-up, dust with oatmeal and brush off after an hour or so.

Flat or matted suede

Can be restored with a gentle rub from an emery board. Use a suede brush afterwards.

For squeaky boots

Often a good dusting with talcum powder will remedy the problem. If not, try this old-fashioned method: bore a small hole in the middle of the sole, and push in a small piece of a matchstick. Perhaps consider asking a cobbler for his opinion on the matter . . .

Smelly shoes?

Sprinkle a teaspoon of bicarbonate of soda inside and shake around. Leave for a day before wearing again.

Clogged-up shoe brush?
Wash in warm water and a spoonful of washing powder.

Patent leather
Should be cleaned with warm milk then polished with a soft cloth.

Banana skin on brown shoes
Keep brown leather shoes soft and supple by polishing with the inside of a banana skin. Allow shoes to dry, then polish.

Tough leather shoes
Can be softened with castor oil. Apply evenly with a cloth. The oil will be absorbed when heat from the foot warms the leather.

Meths on your socks
Will remove shoe-polish stains. Dab affected area with methylated spirits before laundering. **Warning: Not for nylon.**

Marks on heels
Don't despair; simply reach for a marker pen and get colouring in.

Wellingtons wet inside?

Try using a hairdryer.

Supple patent shoes

Will stay that way if you give them an occasional rub with Vaseline or olive oil.

Will It Come Out? Stains

The Rules

Treat stains before the washing machine makes things worse – food and body-fluid stains will become further engrained in hot water. Many a stain can be removed with a good soak in cold water.

Test your stain remover first

If you do need to use a solvent, make sure it won't damage your fabric by testing it on a hidden area.

A stain should leave the way it came

If possible, apply your stain remover to the reverse of the fabric. This avoids pushing the stain further through the material.

AVOID STAINED COLLARS IN THE FIRST PLACE

Wipe your neck with a little rubbing alcohol before getting dressed.

A to Z of Stain Removal

Adhesives

The key to removing glue is trying to do so before it sets.
Here's a quick guide to different glues and how you may
be able to remove them. Techniques are for washable
fabrics, carpets and upholstery, unless stated otherwise.

▶ Cellulose-based adhesives on washable fabrics: Rinse in
  cold water, then wash in biological detergent and rinse.

▶ Epoxy resin: Methylated spirits should provide the
  solution.

▶ PVA wood glue: On washable fabrics: Remove excess
  with damp cloth, then apply neat washing-up liquid.
  Wash as usual. For carpets and upholstery, use methylated spirits.

▶ Superglue: This type of glue is activated by water,
  therefore water can help to dissolve it. Saturate a
  cloth in water, and apply to area until glue loosens.
  Take great care with this – superglue on hands or
  eyes is not fun. Don't panic if eyes or fingers do
  become stuck – a damp cotton bud held over the eye
  should unstick it.

▶ And remember, if all else fails, many adhesive manu-

facturers make product-specific solvents. Don't forget
to make that phone call before giving up hope!

Ballpoint pen

Dip a cloth in dry cleaning solvent and sponge on. Apply
solution of washing-up liquid in water (one teaspoon per
half-pint (300 millilitres)), and rinse. It's worth knowing
that hairspray will remove ballpoint pen from vinyl
furniture.

Blood

Soak for an hour in cold salty water, then rinse in unsalted
water and wash as usual. For older bloodstains soak
overnight in a solution of biological washing powder
before washing.

Beer

Use a towel or kitchen roll to soak up as much as possible,
then dab area with a mixture of a teaspoon of washing-up
liquid and a pint (600 millilitres) of warm water. Dry with
kitchen roll, then rinse with cold water.

Candle wax on clothes

Remove as much wax as possible by hand. Place an old,
yet clean, cloth over your ironing board, and lay the fabric

(stain side up) on top. Place a brown paper bag over the
wax, and iron over bag at medium heat without steam.
The wax will soften and stick to the paper. Keep moving
the bag until all the wax has melted onto it. Remove any
residue with dry-cleaning solvent, then wash as usual.

Candle wax on furniture and upholstery

Scrape off as much as possible with a knife, being careful
not to rub any wax in as you do so. Place a double layer of
newspaper over the wax and pass over an iron on a low
setting for 5–10 seconds. Repeat if necessary with fresh
paper.

Chewing gum

Place item in a plastic bag and freeze for twelve hours. Then
use a blunt knife to scrape as much gum as possible from
the garment. Rub in some washing-up liquid and a dash of
white vinegar before washing as normal. For carpets, remove
as much as possible with a knife, then press a plastic bag
filled with ice cubes onto the residue – the thinner the bag
the better. Once frozen, the gum will be easier to snap off.

Chocolate

Use a blunt knife to scrape away as much as you can.
Sponge non-washables with warm water and a little dry

laundry solvent (available as bars). For washable
garments, pour boiling water from a height on the reverse
of the stain. Rinse and apply laundry solvent to any
residue.

Cigarette burns on carpet

Rub charred bits gently with sandpaper. Pour a few drops
of detergent onto stain and dust with borax until covered.
Rub in well, and leave for ten minutes. Sponge clean with
a damp cloth.

Cigarette burns on polished wood

Rub gently with extra-fine sandpaper or steel wool.
Massage in a few drops of linseed oil and leave for a day
before polishing as usual.

Coffee

Coffee stains on washable items should be sponged with
warm water and borax. Dampen old stains and cover with
dry borax. Pour hot water through fabric. For carpets and
upholstery, soak with soda water and dry with kitchen roll
before sponging with a solution of half a teaspoon of
detergent and half a teaspoon of white vinegar in half a
litre of warm water.

Cream or milk

A pint of warm washing-up liquid solution should hit the spot.

Deodorant stains

Rub white vinegar or lemon juice into the stain and leave for half an hour. Then wash on the hottest setting the item can withstand. For deeply ingrained, hard deodorant stains, dab with dry-cleaning fluid and rinse. As a last resort, try household ammonia.

Fountain pen ink

Act immediately! Cover stain with salt while ink is still wet, and remove salt (scraping with a butter knife works well) as it takes on the colour of the ink. Repeat this until no more ink will be absorbed, then rub spot with a slice of lemon. Soak in milk before washing as usual.

Fruit stains

Fruit stains on linen and cotton may be removed by the following method. Tie up some cream of tartar in the stained area, and let it boil in soapy water for a few minutes. Wash and rinse the article in clear water and the stain will be gone.

Grass

Again, time is of the essence. For cottons, soak in a
solution of one part ammonia, two parts methylated
spirits, and three parts hot water. Rinse and wash in the
usual manner. On synthetics, try methylated spirits with a
teaspoon or two of eucalyptus oil. For woollens, dampen
the stain and spread on a layer of toothpaste. Rinse with
warm water after half an hour. Methylated spirits will
work for carpets.

Grease spots

Can be removed from a woollen skirt or jacket, by dipping
a flannel cloth in petrol and rubbing the spot gently for
the briefest of time, without damaging the dye or the cloth
in the slightest. Alternatively, dip a piece of flannel in a
little ammonia and water, and rub the spot.

Grease spills

On fabric, carpet and upholstery, apply blotting paper (or
kitchen roll) immediately, then dust with talcum powder
or salt. Leave for a couple of hours, and vacuum. For dry
grease, mix salt and dry-cleaning solvent into a paste. Rub
into stain, leave for an hour, then brush off. Vacuum once
completely dry. On wood, cover a spillage immediately
with cold water, then scrape up as much as possible using

a knife. Sponge varnished wood with warm soapy water
(add a tablespoon of white spirit, if possible). If wood is
unvarnished, adding two tablespoons of washing soda to
warm water will provide a highly effective solution.

Ink (general)

Rub tomato on the stain and it may disappear. Then wash
in lukewarm water. Alternatively, dip the stained part into
cold water and then cover with salt. Pour the juice of one
lemon over the salt and leave for two hours. Then wash as
usual.

Lipstick on your collar

Scrape any excess off with a knife before rubbing in some
Vaseline or shampoo, which will loosen the stain. Works
on generally grimy collars too.

Make-up

Dab with dry-cleaning solvent, then wash with soap and
water.

Mascara

Sponge with a little washing-up liquid followed by a few
drops of household ammonia. Rinse thoroughly.

Mud or soot

Sprinkle salt on muddy footprints at once. Leave for half an hour, then vacuum.

Paint

Water-based paints should respond well to being wiped with a warm damp cloth. Oil-based paints should be dabbed with white spirit. Remove stubborn paint from clothes with equal parts ammonia and turpentine. Saturate the spot three or four times, then wash off with soapsuds. Rinse well in clear water.

Red wine

Treat as quickly as possible.

For carpets: Cover stain with salt, wait until salt has absorbed colour, and scrape off. Repeat until no more colour is absorbed. Rinse with plenty of water.

For clothes: Soak in soda water if possible, if not plain cold water. Then wash as usual.

If the wine has dried, apply a solution of equal parts glycerine and warm water, and leave for fifteen minutes. Rinse with cold water.

Shoe polish

Polish on clothing should come off with methylated spirits. Hold a clean cloth under the stain (to prevent it spreading) and dab with cotton wool soaked in meths. Dab carpets with methylated spirits or dry-cleaning fluid.

Tar-stained garments

Rub well with butter and lather with soap, then rinse and dry. If this does not work, lighter fuel, eucalyptus oil, butter and Brasso will all help soften and remove. Try them alone, or in combination, then wash as usual. The same treatment will work for carpets – shampoo afterwards.

Tea

Pour boiling water through the cloth while the stain is still fresh to remove the discoloration. Then wash as normal. For tea on a carpet, treat as mud, i.e. sprinkle with salt and vacuum after half an hour.

Urine

Treat immediately. If urine is left too long, professional cleaning will be required.

For washable fabrics: cover area with salt, then rinse thoroughly in cold water and wash as usual. For stubborn

stains, apply household ammonia. Rinse off and douse
with vinegar before washing again.

For carpets (and other non-washable fabrics): blot
with kitchen roll and apply salt. Brush off, rinse, and apply
carpet or upholstery shampoo.

Underarm stains

Dissolve ten aspirins in a cup of warm water and soak
underarm area for half an hour. Discard aspirin water to
ensure nobody drinks it.

Oh No, Not the Wallpaper!

Dirty wallpaper is as unappealing to you as it is to your
guests. In general, non-washable wallpaper should be
maintained with the soft brush attachment of a vacuum
cleaner, while washable wallpaper should (obviously) be
washed. When a rogue stain appears, deal with it at once
using the following techniques:

For dirt stains

Many incidental stains will take kindly to a gentle rubbing
with a piece of stale white bread (which can't be said for
many things).

For greasy stains

Place kitchen roll over stain and iron lightly. For heavier stains, mix cornflour and water into a paste and apply to the spot. Leave to dry then carefully brush off.

For ink

Nip this in the bud as quick as you can. Dab with a tissue, followed by a gentle dab with cotton wool soaked in clear vinegar – be sure not to rub, as this could worsen the stain. Try methylated spirits as a last resort.

For pencil marks

Use a pencil rubber. Makes sense, really.

If you need to patch wallpaper, use a torn rather than cut-out piece. To remove stained or damaged paper, spray with water and gently ease off. When you paste the new torn patch on, the feathered edges will blend in better than on a straight cut piece.

Life is Hard Enough

General Advice to Make Things Easier

Winter warmth

Your room will stay warmer for longer if curtains are drawn at dusk during the cold months.

Sellotape

Place a small button at the end of the roll. Saves time, frustration and your fingernails. To loosen Sellotape that is stuck, steam for a couple of seconds and all will be well.

Smooth runners

Rub furniture polish on metal curtain rails to prevent rust and ensure your curtains glide easily. For non-metallic rails, talcum powder works wonders.

Separate stacked glasses

Without breaking them. Place the bottom glass in hot water and pour cold water into the top glass. Twist gently and the glasses should come apart safely.

Free your salt

Add a dried pea or two to the cellar to ensure your salt keeps flowing freely. A few grains of rice will also do the job.

Don't store wine glasses upside down

As they will develop a musty smell. Far better to store them upright, and deal with any dust by rinsing and polishing before use.

Slipping mats and rugs

Glue on pieces of foam rubber, or sew on washers from jam jars.

Can't unscrew a bottletop or jam jar?

If a cloth doesn't work, gripping with sandpaper could be the answer.

Glow-in-the-dark keys

Make your keys easier to find in a bag by sticking a quantity of fluorescent tape to them. This will save an awful lot of fumbling in the dark.

Rub apple slices on your windscreen

To prevent it icing over in winter. A cut potato works, too.

A mislaid corkscrew

Is no reason to panic. Locate a reasonably long screw (dismantle furniture if really desperate) and twist into cork. Tie a piece of string or a shoelace to the screw head, and pull!

Before a barbeque

Rub the grill with oil. This will stop your sausages from sticking and make cleaning a breeze. Use leftover ground coffee for cleaning.

Condensation-free windows

Are easily achieved. A small cup of salt placed by the window will soak up moisture and enable you to keep a closer eye on the neighbours.

Broken glass

Can be easily picked up using one side of a thick slice of bread. No need for butter, and don't forget to discard immediately. Alternatively, moisten some newspapers and press it onto the shards.

Tighten a cane chair

Cane and wicker chairs can lose their shape over time. To restore tautness, sponge chairs with a solution of hot water and baking soda. Soak up excess water with a clean cloth, then leave in the sun to dry.

Dropped an egg on the floor?

Use a baster to suck up most of it to save you from
wrestling with a slimy mess.

Remove a broken light bulb with newspaper

Wearing gloves, screw up a couple of newspaper sheets
and apply the wad to the glass. Turn anticlockwise, and the
bulb should come out easily.

Hold a small nail with a hairpin

When hammering in tiny nails, make the job less fiddly
(and guard against hammered fingers) by placing each
nail in the bend of a hairclip. Remove before the final
whack!

Hairclips also make great bookmarks

They don't fall out!

Lost your cork? Don't lose your bottle

If you need to re-cork a bottle but have no cork, warm a
candle until soft, wrap it in a piece of kitchen roll and
insert into bottle.

Smear Vaseline around a tight ring

This may well help it slide from your finger. Try running your hand under cold water too, as warm hands will shrink a little when cold.

Wear socks on your knees

For handy knee pads when gardening or cleaning, cut the toes off old socks and pull a little higher up the leg!

Keep your feet dry

Unless your boots are one hundred per cent waterproof, try the following before a walk in wet weather or snow: after putting on your socks, slip your feet into a plastic bag before donning your boots.

Wear socks over shoes

When painting, slip an old pair of socks over your shoes to guard against stray drops of paint.

Toilet roll tubes for cables

Keep your cardboard tubes from toilet and kitchen rolls for neat storage of cables, extension leads and other cords for appliances you are not using. Label the tubes accordingly, and feel smug that you no longer have a drawer full of unravelling cables. . . .

Keep charcoal in your wardrobe

A damp wardrobe spells bad news for clothes. For a home-made dehumidifier, place several charcoal briquettes in a coffee tin, and pierce several holes in the lid.

Silence a dripping tap

Tying a cloth around the spout of a dripping tap won't solve the problem, but it will let you get a good night's sleep. Call the plumber in the morning!

Alternative to stamp licking

If you have many stamps to stick, save your tongue and instead place half a dozen ice cubes in a bowl. Rub each stamp on a cube.

Spy on your freezer using a coin

Before you go away for any length of time, place a penny on top of an ice cube. If it is still there when you get back, it is most likely that no power failures occurred. Even if there was a brief interruption in supply, it did not last long enough for your freezer to defrost and spoil your food.

Mothballs in a toolbox

A handful of mothballs placed in a toolbox will prevent tools from rusting.

Grease on the patio

Grease on patios and driveways should be covered in a generous amount of dishwasher powder and left to sit for a few hours. Rinse off with a kettle of boiling water. Repeat if necessary. Make sure no dogs or cats are around, though. Poisonous if licked off paws.

How to find a contact lens

Cover the head of your vacuum cleaner with an old pair of tights, and vacuum the area where you lost your contact. The suction will pick up the lens, and the tights will prevent it from disappearing.

Keep sleeping bags fresh

Pop a fabric-softener sheet inside your sleeping bags when not in use.

Hairdryer as bellows

A hairdryer on low is an excellent way to get your fire going.

To make sure an envelope cannot be steamed open
Apply nail varnish to the flap. It dries very quickly and, unlike most envelope gum, will not soften when steamed.

Leave valuables with a friend or a bank
It's a good idea to leave valuable jewellery somewhere outside of your house when you go on holiday.

Prevent damp beds
If you are going to be away for a while, your bed may become damp. Guard against this by leaving a blanket on top of your bed. Everything underneath it will remain dry for three to four weeks.

A strap around a suitcase
Protects it from opening, makes it easy to identify and gives opportunist thieves less time to open it up.

Postage stamps in the fridge
If stamps are stuck together, put them in the fridge for a few minutes and they will come apart.

Protect a parcel
Rub a candle over the address on a parcel to protect it from rain.

Don't steam a stamp to remove it

A rub with lighter fuel on the envelope's inside (behind the stamp, of course) is much quicker.

Box-packing gem

When packing cardboard boxes you will open later (e.g. when moving house), place a length of string underneath any tape – leave a few centimetres hanging over the edge of the box and you will be able to rip up the tape without the need for a knife.

A stiff lock

Will often loosen if you rub a lead pencil on the key.

Cork stuck in the bottle?

Pour boiling water onto a towel and, once cool enough to touch, wrap around the neck of your bottle. The glass will expand with the heat, and the cork should come out with the aid of a corkscrew.

For instant real coffee

When you have made a large amount of very strong coffee, freeze it in ice-cube trays. When you need your next caffeine hit, simply add boiling water to a couple of the cubes.

Freeze your cling film
It will unroll and tear much more easily, and will stick to bowls, but not to itself.

Store newspaper cuttings
Newsprint will fade over time. Keep important cuts in polyester film folders, and make sure the paper behind them is alkaline buffered. Store in acid-free boxes away from sunlight and heat.

Moss on the patio?
Pour apple cider vinegar over it and leave for a couple of hours before rinsing with warm water.

Turn a wheelbarrow into a makeshift barbecue
Pour charcoal into the bottom of barrow, and place an oven rack across the barrow. Not suitable for wooden or plastic models . . .

Keep a plastic bag in your handbag
A good leather handbag should never get wet. A stowed plastic bag can be whipped out and used as a cover when you are caught in the rain.

Sellotape your car lock

To prevent it freezing. Or stick a fridge magnet over it.

Unclog an aerosol

Spray cans sometimes clog up way before they are empty. Remove the nozzle and soak in boiling water for a few minutes to get it back in working order.

Don't discard your ballpoint pen

A seemingly dry ballpoint pen is often merely clogged. Try running it under a hot tap for a few minutes – more often than not the ink will soon flow again.

A bolt that won't budge

A few drops of Coca-Cola or ammonia should loosen it after a few seconds.

Sponge-mop lifespan

Lengthen your mophead's life by popping a plastic bag over it after rinsing thoroughly in cold salty water. Secure with a rubber band. This simple effort will prevent the sponge from drying out and cracking, adding many months to its life.

Cancel the milk

And the newspapers in person before you go on holiday. A
note on the doorstep can fall into the wrong hands.
Returning to a burgled house is a terrible end to a
relaxing break.

Unfreeze a lock with a hot key

Heat your key with a match or lighter and insert into lock.

Leave your address off luggage labels

Use your work address so potential burglars have nothing
to go on . . .

Messages on the door

Place notes for tradesmen, milkmen, postmen (or any
other men or women!) inside a plastic bag. Secure with a
pin or peg, and the weather will not wash your words
away.

Long-life rubber gloves

Turn Marigolds inside out and stick a strip of plaster
across the top of each finger. Particularly handy if you
have long nails.

Sticky door

If a door keeps sticking, rub the edge with chalk, then close it. Reopen, and inspect the frame for signs of chalk – it will be marked at the sticking point. Now reach for the sandpaper . . .

Home-made portable barbecue

For picnics, use a biscuit tin and a grill pan grid instead of a shop-bought barbecue.

Stained Thermos flask

A tablespoon of good old bicarbonate of soda, a top-up with boiling water, and an overnight wait is all you need to put things right between you and your Thermos.

For a cooler bed in summer

In the hot summer months, sprinkle some baby powder between your sheets for a cool feeling in bed.

Free, strong elastic

Before throwing out old rubber gloves, cut strips from the cuffs to make very useful, tough elastic bands.

Christmas Hints

Blowdry your turkey
A hairdryer can speed up the defrosting time if your
turkey timings are a little off.

Soak dried fruit and peel
A few minutes in boiling water will improve the plumpness
and taste, and soften a little.

Mince pie cheat
Pass off shop-bought mince pies as your own by lifting
their lids and giving each pie a squirt of brandy before
popping them in the oven.

Keep your nuts cool
Put nuts away at night, as they will turn rancid quickly if
left out in the heat.

Avoid cracks in mulled wine glasses
Hold a metal spoon in each glass before you
pour.

Posh up your Christmas cake

To make a cheaper cake taste rather more expensive, use a skewer to poke a dozen or so holes into the cake. Pour a few drops of decent brandy into each hole about two weeks before Christmas Day. Turn cake over and repeat five days later, and repeat the process two more times before the 25th arrives.

Dry Christmas puddings

Adding cold tea to your pudding mix prevents it drying out, and will enhance its colour too.

Evenly boiled puddings

To guarantee an even boil, criss-cross a few skewers at the bottom of the pan.

Wrap your Christmas tree in a bed sheet

Christmas is over, and it's time to drag the tree outside. Wrap it up in an old towel or sheet first, and save the floor from all those pine needles.

Cut up your cards

Cut out pretty designs from this year's Christmas cards and use them as labels for next year's presents.

To keep the brandy burning

Heat the plate the pudding sits on, not just the brandy.

Leave salt in your cellar

To eradicate damp. Divide a kilo of kitchen salt into
four tins (one for each corner of the cellar), and leave
until salt is saturated. Dry salt in the oven and replace.
Within a few days, you should have a much drier
cellar.

Unstick a stopper

If your decanter stopper is stuck, tap around it gently
using a similar glass stopper.

Musty, smelly flasks

Are a pain when you're getting ready for an excursion.
This situation will arise no longer if you always leave a
few sugar lumps in your dry flask. The stopper should be
loose enough to allow air flow.

Avoid frozen waste pipes

By keeping in bath and sink plugs during cold snaps –
this prevents drips of water getting into pipes and
freezing.

Don't sleep through an alarm

An alarm clock on a metal tray makes a lot more noise!

Favourite vinyl record warped?

Don't despair. Place between two sheets of glass, wait for a sunny day, and leave outside for a few hours.

To get a cork back in

Give it a soak in boiling water. After a few minutes it will be nicely malleable.

Vaseline on a hinge

Should stop it squeaking. So should a good rub with a lead pencil, or a few drops of washing-up liquid. Of course, there's always oil . . .

Run central heating in summer

But only for a few minutes every week or so. This helps ensure it will run smoothly when the cold weather creeps in.

Pet Corner

Cat pills in butter

Awkward cats who won't take their medicine can be
tricked into it. Crush any pills between two spoons and
mix the powder into a teaspoon of butter. Spread the
mixture on the cat's legs, and he will lick it off none the
wiser.

Puppies knawing your furniture?

Rub the legs with a little clove oil. The taste is guaranteed
to stop any tail wagging, and should prevent them going
back for more.

Home-made dog shampoo

Mix one part Dettol and two parts washing-up liquid
with three parts water. Will keep for ever! If you don't
want to get your pooch wet (e.g. during winter months),
give him a rub with bicarbonate of soda, then brush
out.

Pets with bad breath

Rub a damp cloth dipped in bicarbonate of soda over the
animal's teeth.

Stop cats from scratching

Double-sided Sellotape will ensure cats do not sit on your favourite furniture, or use it as a scratching post – they can't bear the stickiness on their paws. Works on kitchen surfaces too.

Is your hamster dead, or just cold?

A hamster will go to sleep when particularly cold or chilled, and may appear dead. Do not give up hope until you have moved it to a warm place, wrapped it in a woolly sock and given it a gentle warm-up with the hairdryer. Hamsters can also go rigid and collapse when scared or stressed – wait a few days before the burial!

A clock for a puppy

Keep a young puppy calm when he or she has been removed from a litter by placing a ticking clock and a hot-water bottle under a thick blanket in the basket.

Rubber gloves remove pet hair

Don a rubber glove and give your furniture a good rub-down. Rub in one direction and you will end up with a ball of hair that is easily removed.

Don't smash the ice on a fishpond

The impact sends shockwaves through the water that may kill the fish. Instead, sit a hot pan or kettle on top of the ice until it melts.

When the Cat's Away
Keeping Household Pests at Bay

Ants hate chalk

So they won't cross a chalk line. Locate the point where
ants are entering your house, draw a line, and they
shouldn't bother you any more. Sometimes it's good to
live and let live. If you must ruin their fun, locate the nest
and cover in a couple of kettle's worth of boiling water.

Bees and wasps

If you are picnicking or in the garden, take a jar half filled
with water and a spoonful of jam and position it a few
metres away from you. The bees and wasps will be far
more interested in this than in you. Never attempt to
eliminate nests – leave this to a professional.

Cockroaches

Love warm, dark corners, especially wood and plaster.
Scattering pinches of washing soda will banish them from
such places. Alternatively, mix one cup of well-pounded
plaster of Paris with two cups of oatmeal and quarter of a
cup of sugar. Distribute the mixture around the floor,
particularly in those corners. As a last resort, share your
red wine with the little devils. Pour into saucers and leave
under kitchen cabinets – the roaches will get drunk and
drown.

Earwigs

Love plants. To keep earwigs out of your house, keep
creeper plants and tendrils away from your windows and
doors. A sprinkle of insecticide on your outside window
frames will also help. No need to take any precautions
around your ears.

Fleas

Treat cats and dogs with commercial products. The same
goes for carpets. Alternatively, for a home-made flea trap,
fill a shallow dish with water and place a bright table
lamp (ideally 100 watts) over the pan. Leave overnight —
the fleas will be attracted to the lamp and end up in the
water. Change water every day and repeat until the fleas
jump no more. Mothballs in your vacuum bag will also
help to kill fleas in your carpet.

Flies

Hang bunches of dried lavender or fresh stinging nettles in
rooms (by open windows and doors is best), and include
then in flower arrangements, to keep flies at bay.
Alternatively, mix a teaspoon of black pepper, two
teaspoons of brown sugar and two tablespoons of cream.
Leave mixture out in a shallow dish, and flies will keep
their distance.

Fly stains

To deter flies from dirtying windows, mirrors and other glass items, polish with a small amount of Brasso. Flies abhor it.

Hairspray for flies and wasps

Hairspray locks wings in place and puts a stop to the buzzing very quickly!

Keep squirrels off your bird feeder

By greasing the pole with Vaseline. Not only will this ensure squirrels slip off the pole, it will provide endless moments of amusement for you.

Mice

To prevent mice entering the house, plug all holes in floor boards or walls with wire wool. Also, mice greatly dislike the smell of peppermint. Sprinkle a little peppermint oil round their haunts and holes to successfully keep these pests away, and push a cork into any mousehole you come across. Fresh raw meat and chocolate are the best baits for mousetraps. Also, consider getting (or borrowing) a cat – the best mouse deterrent there is. For a humane trap, butter a large bowl, and leave some cheese in the bottom. Stack some books next to the bowl (to make a

little staircase); a mouse will be able to climb in but not
out! Take the bowl outside to free it.

Mosquito repellent

Strain a peeled and puréed cucumber into an ice-cube tray
and freeze. Rub skin with ice cubes before you leave the
house, and the mosquitoes will look elsewhere.

Moths

Fill small bags of muslin with cedar-wood shavings, sew
them up, and place them in drawers and cupboards.
Alternatively, strew pimento berries or musk-plant seeds
among clothes and blankets. If moths have already laid
their eggs in woollen articles, put the infested items in a
plastic bag and put in the freezer overnight before
washing or dry cleaning. Moth eggs in a carpet can be
eradicated with a hot iron and a cold damp cloth. Iron
cloth over affected areas.

DIY FLYTRAP

Mix a pint (600 millilitres) of milk, 100 grams
sugar and 50 grams pepper. Heat in a pan and
simmer for fifteen minutes. Leave mixture around
your house in shallow dishes – flies will adore their
drink, but also drown in it.

Give slugs beer

Fill a couple of bowls with your finest ale and leave it out for the slugs. They'll drink themselves to death – from drowning, not drunkenness.

Pepper your bugs

Sprinkle a combination of black pepper and flour in and around plants to keep bugs at bay.

Weevils hate garlic

Pop a clove or two in with your dried beans, pulses and grains, and weevils will not pay them a visit.

Woodworm

Can spread easily, so always check second-hand furniture before bringing it into your home. The telltale signs are pin-sized holes surrounded by fine sawdust – this could be on the floor too. Apply liquid paraffin to all holes, then spread melted beeswax to seal the holes. Allow to dry, rub down and polish.

Little Bundles of Joy?

Nursery and Childcare Hints

Fun ice cubes

Keep the plastic holding trays from chocolate boxes, fill
with water and freeze for more interesting cubes. Great
for kids' parties.

Home-made modelling dough

Mix a cup of salt, two cups of flour, four tablespoons each
of cream of tartar and vegetable oil and a cup of water
until smooth. Cook in a saucepan and stir constantly until
the dough leaves the side of the pan and forms a ball.
Split the mixture up into several parts, and add different
food colourings. Knead well, and store for up to a week in
polythene bags.

Medicine

To give a spoonful of Calpol or other medicine to a child,
place the point of the spoon against the roof of his or her
mouth. Given this way, the child will not choke or be able
to reject the medicine.

Ink on a doll's face

This all-too-common toy affliction can be cured. For a
brighter Barbie (or a cleaner Ken) rub face with butter,
and leave in sunlight for a couple of days. . . .

An ice cube

Placed in the mouth will numb the tongue and make unpleasant medicine easier to swallow. It will also numb an area of skin surrounding a splinter in need of removal.

Childproof your kitchen

With toddlers around, it's a good idea to stretch elastic bands between handles on cupboards and drawers. This will prevent prying fingers making any dangerous discoveries.

Nightmares

Never be cross or impatient if your child has a nightmare – it will only make matters worse. He or she may seem to be awake, but is most likely still half-asleep and will be further traumatised by cross words. Try to help prevent nightmares by giving a light evening meal, a relaxed bath time, and a soothing bedtime story. Do not let the child read on his or her own, or watch television just before bedtime.

For gigantic bubbles

To create supersized bubbles, pour your bubble solution into a wide tray and dip a wire coat hanger into it. Do not blow, but pull slowly through the air. (There's no need to buy bubble solution – washing-up liquid in water does the job brilliantly.)

Egg boxes

Make great paint pots for a creative session with multiple colours, and are easy to dispose of when tidying up your children's mess.

Chewing gum in hair

Ease off gently with baby oil and cotton wool. Alternatively, massage your locks with peanut butter and comb out. Don't forget to shampoo afterwards.

Buy nappies in bulk

Cut out the middle man, and order nappies in bulk from local suppliers. Consider clubbing together with other mums to place a big order.

For a child-friendly piano

Piano lids can crush little fingers. Prevent musical disasters by attaching a cork to each end of the keyboard.

Glow-in-the-dark light switches

Paint around electric switches in children's rooms with fluorescent paint so that it is easier for them to get up during the night.

Don't bring sand back from the beach

Take a large mesh bag on a day at the seaside. Throw all washable items in at the end of the day. That way, bottles, buckets, sunglasses and shells can all be washed off in the sea, or under a tap, before you get back in the car.

Make a huge piece of chalk

Save up twenty eggshells (washing them well as you go along) and crush into a fine powder with a mortar and pestle. Mix three teaspoons each of hot water and flour to form a paste, and mix well with the eggshells. Fill a cardboard toilet-roll tube with the mixture, and after four or five days your giant chalk will be ready!

Washing-up liquid at bathtime

A squirt or two will provide some fun bubbles and stop scum marks forming too. This makes for easier cleaning.

Cut up your gloves

The fingers of old gloves make great finger puppets — decorate with cotton, buttons, paper and glue.

Name-tape trick

If your children have different initials, order a batch of name tapes with each initial at different ends of the surname. That way you can tuck one end away when sewing on.

Bathroom toy storage

Keep bath toys in a mesh bag with a drawstring. This allows you to rinse them all at once after use, and helps to keep your bathroom clutter free.

Hidden patches

Sew patches on the insides of elbows and knees in clothing – they work just as well as patches on the outside, and your children won't feel self-conscious when they leave the house!

Talcum powder at the beach

Take talcum powder to the beach. It's perfect for dusting damp feet with before you get back in the car, or walk inside – the sand falls right off.

Take down your towel rail!

If you have a large family, the chances are there isn't much room in your bathroom to hang up towels. Consider removing towel rails and putting up some hooks – one for each member of the family.

Sandpaper shoes

The soles of new boots and shoes often benefit from a light sandpapering to prevent slipping when first worn.

Dampen shoelaces

Giving shoelaces a light rub with a wet cloth before tying will ensure they remain 'done up' for longer.

Rubber band around a glass

Wrapping a wide elastic band around a cup or glass can improve a young child's chances of holding on to it!

Make Do and Mend
Money-Saving Tips

Put old clocks in the oven

But only if they have stopped working. Old wooden clocks which appear to have ticked their final tock may well come back to life after a gentle warm in a low oven.

Warped wooden breadboards

Need not be shown the dustbin. Place them on a flat surface (Convex side down) and cover with a wet tea towel. Leave for a day or two.

Old pyjama bottoms

Cut the legs off for a super pair of makeshift ironing-board covers.

Make your radiator hotter for free

Cut a piece of rigid insulation to the same size as your radiator (so that it can slide behind – bear the brackets in mind) and cover it in aluminium foil. Place out of sight between radiator and wall, and you will notice the difference.

Wash out your washing-up-liquid bottle

And fill it with oil for a handy, non-drip oil dispenser.

No more rusty pins

Stuff your pincushions with used and dried coffee grounds. The coffee will prevent rust for evermore.

Old net curtains

Are very handy if you screw them up into bunches, tie with string and use as bath cleaners. They are abrasive enough to remove grime, but will not scratch.

Make holes in jar lids

To turn your jar into a water dredger or water sprinkler by piercing small holes in the lids. Use a bradawl, or a very slim screwdriver, to do this.

Soap saver

Cut the top off an old washing-up-liquid bottle and store soap end-bits inside. Add a drop of boiling water each time you add more soap, and drop a teaspoon of glycerine in now and again. Stir often. Once the bottle is full, give contents a final stir and leave to rest. Once contents have set, peel away bottle and slice up into bars.

Home-made firelighters

Save all paper (newspapers, magazines, old letters) to recycle as fuel bricks. Fill the bath with water and soak a mass of paper until it is reduced to pulp. Tear it into strips before squeezing hard into tight, cricket ball-sized balls. Leave to dry in a warm place.

Burn dried potato peelings

Your fire will burn more evenly and accumulate less soot. Remove soot from your chimney by regularly throwing a handful of the following mixture on a brightly burning fire: 450 grams flowers of sulphur and 225 grams powdered saltpetre (potassium nitrate). This will save you money on expensive flue cleaners.

Saving used matches

Will eventually provide some excellent kindling. To make a fire last, fill a damp egg box (cardboard, not plastic) with chips and dust from your coal cellar or bunker. This will burn steadily and slowly for hours when placed in the centre of the fire.

Don't waste money on sugar

All sugar is the same, so there's no need to buy caster and icing sugar separately. You can easily grind granulated sugar into the required grade in a grinder or your liquidiser – a couple of seconds for caster sugar, ten seconds for icing sugar.

Useful Addresses

Products and Suppliers:

Ammonia, household – hardware stores, Boots the Chemist or online

Boracic (Boric acid) powder – www.mistralni.co.uk

Borax – Boots the Chemist or www.baldwins.co.uk

Caustic soda – Boots the Chemist

Chalk, powdered – online at www.petplanet.co.uk

Charcoal, ground – www.baldwins.co.uk

Cod Liver oil – local chemists or online

Epsom salts – local chemists and www.epsomsalt.co.uk

Eucalyptus oil – www.enaissance.co.uk

Flowers of sulpur – www.morgan111morgan.com

French chalk powder (talc) – www.industrial-markers.co.uk

Lanolin – www.baldwins.co.uk

Linseed oil – hardware stores, or www.wood-finishes-direct.com

Menthol crystals – local chemists

Methylated spirits – hardware stores

Orris root – health food shops or www.steenbergs.co.uk

Paraffin – hardware stores and camping shops

Plaster of Paris – art and craft shops or www.maragon.co.uk

Pumice, powdered – www.agwoodcare.co.uk and www.aromantic.co.uk

Rubbing alcohol (surgical spirit) – local chemist or www.expresschemist.co.uk

Saltpetre (potassium nitrate) – www.legendsofavalon.co.uk

Turpentine – hardware and DIY shops

Washing soda/household soda – supermarkets

Acknowledgements

Many thanks to Rosemary Davidson at Square Peg for commissioning this book and demonstrating your hairdressing skills on Mark. Also, thanks to Helena Masters for a wonderful cover design. We are thoroughly indebted to our mums for their help and advice, along with countless books and web pages, of which there are far too many to mention.

Index